IT HAPPENED TO ME

Series Editor: Arlene Hirschfelder

Books in the It Happened to Me series are designed for inquisitive teens digging for answers about certain illnesses, social issues, or lifestyle interests. Whether you are deep into your teen years or just entering them, these books are gold mines of up-to-date information, riveting teen views, and great visuals to help you figure out stuff. Besides special boxes highlighting singular facts, each book is enhanced with the latest reading list, websites, and an index. Perfect for browsing, there's loads of expert information by acclaimed writers to help parents, guardians, and librarians understand teen illness, tough situations, and lifestyle choices.

1. *Learning Disabilities: The Ultimate Teen Guide,* by Penny Hutchins Paquette and Cheryl Gerson Tuttle, 2003.
2. *Epilepsy: The Ultimate Teen Guide,* by Kathlyn Gay and Sean McGarrahan, 2002.
3. *Stress Relief: The Ultimate Teen Guide,* by Mark Powell, 2002.
4. *Making Sexual Decisions: The Ultimate Teen Guide*, by L. Kris Gowen, Ph.D., 2003.
5. *Asthma: The Ultimate Teen Guide*, by Penny Hutchins Paquette, 2003.
6. *Cultural Diversity: Conflicts and Challenges: The Ultimate Teen Guide*, by Kathlyn Gay, 2003.
7. *Diabetes: The Ultimate Teen Guide,* by Katherine J. Moran, 2004.
8. *When Will I Stop Hurting? Teens, Loss, and Grief: The Ultimate Teen Guide*, by Edward Myers, 2004.
9. *Volunteering: The Ultimate Teen Guide*, by Kathlyn Gay, 2004.
10. *Organ Transplant: A Survival Guide for Recipients and Their Families: The Ultimate Teen Guide*, by Tina P. Schwartz, 2005.

11. *Medications: The Ultimate Teen Guide*, by Cheryl Gerson Tuttle, 2005.
12. *Image and Identity: Becoming the Person You Are*, by L. Kris Gowen, Ph.D., Ed.M., and Molly C. McKenna, Ph.D., 2005.
13. *Apprenticeship*, by Penny Hutchins Paquette, 2005.
14. *Cystic Fibrosis*, by Melanie Ann Apel, 2006.
15. *Religion and Spirituality in America: The Ultimate Teen Guide*, by Kathlyn Gay, 2006.
16. *Gender Identity: The Ultimate Teen Guide*, by Cynthia L. Winfield, 2006.
17. *Physical Disabilities: The Ultimate Teen Guide*, by Denise Thornton, 2007.

Physical Disabilities

The Ultimate Teen Guide

Denise Thornton

It Happened to Me, No. 17

The Scarecrow Press, Inc.
Lanham, Maryland • Toronto • Plymouth, UK
2007

SCARECROW PRESS, INC.

Published in the United States of America
by Scarecrow Press, Inc.
A wholly owned subsidiary of
The Rowman & Littlefield Publishing Group, Inc.
4501 Forbes Boulevard, Suite 200, Lanham, Maryland 20706
www.scarecrowpress.com

Estover Road
Plymouth PL6 7PY
United Kingdom

British Library Cataloguing in Publication Information Available

Library of Congress Cataloging-in-Publication Data

Thornton, Denise, 1949–
Physical disabilities : the ultimate teen guide / Denise Thornton.
p. cm. — (It happened to me ; no. 17)
Includes bibliographical references and index.
ISBN-13: 978-0-8108-5300-3 (hardcover : alk. paper)
ISBN-10: 0-8108-5300-0 (hardcover : alk. paper)
1. Teenagers with disabilities—Juvenile literature. I. Title.
RJ507.H35T56 2007
362.40835--dc22

2006029235

™ The paper used in this publication meets the minimum requirements of American National Standard for Information Sciences—Permanence of Paper for Printed Library Materials, ANSI/NISO Z39.48-1992.
Manufactured in the United States of America.

Contents

Acknowledgments

So many people contributed to creating this book. First, I must thank my husband, Doug Hansmann, for his encouragement, and my daughters, Della and K. J., whose constant support fueled this project.

I am forever indebted to the young adults who opened their hearts to me and breathed live into this project, especially Jackie Barns, Dan Burton, Annie Connor, Shawna Culp, Mich (Michelle) Gerson, Courtney Glodowski, Laura Glowacki, Dave Groesbeck, Carl Hamming, Quinn Haberl, Kathryn Healy, Angela Kuemmel, Michelle Suzanne Maloney, Jessie Martin, Alex McKenzie, Isaac Powell, Katy Sandberg, Matt Scott, Matt Shand, Hannah Thompson, Statia Wilson, and Rebecca Wylie.

I am grateful to all the caring professionals who shared their time and expertise for this project. The Northern Suburban Special Education District, including Karen Noonan, program director; Becki Streit, Low Incidence Cooperative Agreement (LICA) Programs and Services for Students Who Are Deaf and Hard of Hearing; Naomi Hershman, vision coordinator; Barbara Sides, retired occupational and physical therapy coordinator; and Karolyn Berkiel, computer and technology coordinator. Thanks also to Deb Claire and Annie Robertson, accommodations specialists at the McBurney Disability Resource Center of the University of Wisconsin, Madison; Tanya Holton, vice president of development at the National Braille Press; Jackie Pieper and Dan Ferreria of the Great Lakes Adaptive Sports Association;

Melissa Mitchell, outreach and training coordinator for the National Clearinghouse on Disability and Exchange; Eric Lipp, founder and director of Open Doors Organization in Chicago; Mike Froggly, head wheelchair basketball coach at University of Illinois, Urbana-Champaign; Dr. Paul Ponchillia, chairperson of the Department of Blindness and Low Vision Studies of Western Michigan University; Stephanie Moore, director of visual arts, VSA arts, Washington, D.C.; Karen McCulloh, National Organization of Nurses with Disabilities; Karen Black, director of media relations at the National Technical Institute for the Deaf at Rochester Institute of Technology; Michael Hineberg, attendant referral coordinator of IndependenceFirst, Milwaukee, Wisconsin; Cynthia A. Lambert, corporate director for government and community relations at Good Shepherd Rehabilitation Network; Betsy Valnes, executive director of National Youth Leadership Network; and Jennifer McPhail, an organizer with ADAPT.

Special thanks to Angelica Busque, who combined her artistic skill as a fine arts graduate of the School of the Art Institute of Chicago with her experience as a young person with a physical disabilities to create the illustrations for each chapter, and to photographer Tom Olin, who contributed images from his collection of photographs of the demonstrations and civil disobedience that drove the passage in 1990 of the Americans with Disabilities Act.

I also want thank my friends and fellow members of the Society of Children's Book Writers and Illustrators, especially Tina P. Schwartz, who encouraged me to propose this book to my wonderful editor, Arlene Hirschfelder, who has guided me patiently and surely through this project.

Introduction

The issues rising from family, school, and relationships are the same for most teens whether they have physical disabilities or not. This book explores the extra obstacles that confront teens with visual, hearing, and physical disabilities and the ways they surmount them.

My primary sources have been teens and young adults with disabilities. Who knows this topic better than they do? Angela Kuemmel was paralyzed from the shoulders down in a diving accident the day after her fifteenth birthday. She is now working on her Ph.D. in rehabilitation psychology. She was recently selected to be a student representative on the American Psychological Association's Committee on Disability Issues in Psychology.

Quinn Haberl, a sixteen-year-old honor roll student, is blind. When he learned about seeing-eye dogs as a young child, he dreamed of having his own, and he didn't want to wait until he was eighteen to get one. His goal led him on a journey to Quebec, where at age thirteen he proved he was ready to take the responsibility for his own dog. Now he and his family have formed a foundation to make service dogs available to other young people in the United States.

Michelle Maloney was born with severe hearing loss. She navigates the uncertain terrain between the worlds of the hearing and the deaf as she completes a degree that will qualify her to be a rehabilitation counselor in a college setting.

Melissa Mitchell uses a wheelchair because she has cerebral palsy. She began traveling on her own when she was eight.

Now, as outreach and training coordinator for the National Clearinghouse on Disability and Exchange (funded by the U.S. Department of State, Bureau of Cultural and Educational Affairs), she coordinates international travel for people with disabilities.

Dave Groesbeck who has spina bifida, has finally gotten an apartment and job of his own. Isaac Powell, born without a right hand, is learning to explore his feelings through painting icons. Laura Glowacki, who is totally blind, is pursuing a degree in music therapy.

These young people, and many more, have generously opened their hearts to share their frustrations and their dreams. Each person with a disability faces unique challenges—as well as many universal ones. I have organized the book into eight categories: school, tools and technology, transportation and access, sports, the arts, relationships, independence, and advocacy. Each chapter combines the experiences of teens and young adults in all these spheres, with up-to-date information on some of the resources that readers can call on as they follow their own dreams.

Please turn the page—and meet some very cool people.

High School and the Great Beyond

Education is the key to independence and future success. Your education will have a powerful influence on the kind of work you can find and the money you will earn. As a student with a physical disability, you need to take charge of your own education and make sure it is meeting your needs. That is a big responsibility, but there is no way around this one.

"The end of all education should surely be service to others. We cannot seek achievement for ourselves and forget about progress and prosperity for our community. Our ambitions must be broad enough to include the aspirations and needs of others, for their own sake and for our own."

—César Chávez (Called by Senator Robert F. Kennedy "one of the heroic figures of our time," Chávez was a crusader for nonviolent social change.)[1]

HIGH SCHOOL

"There are a lot of challenges, but I'm learning a lot as well," says seventeen-year-old Jessie Martin. Jessie has cerebral palsy. "I have to overcome more, so I learn more. I think that I am more creative than most of my friends because I have to think of different ways to do things."[2]

To be successful as a student with a disability, you have to be creative and resourceful. Some high school students feel they have all the time in the world to think about and plan for the future, but when you have a disability, you need to be thinking two steps ahead all the time.

According to a 2004 survey commissioned by the National Organization on Disability (NOD) students with disabilities are twice as likely to drop out of high school (21 percent versus 10 percent). The same study found that Americans with disabilities are at a critical disadvantage compared to other Americans when it comes to getting a job. Only 35 percent of people with disabilities reported being employed full or part

COURTNEY GLODOWSKI: MAKING ACCOMMODATIONS

Seventeen-year-old Courtney was at the top of her class and played point guard on the basketball team. She played volleyball and ran two miles a day. She was first chair clarinet in the band and sang in the choir. Then she was hit by a bullet when a gun misfired, and she lost her sight.

I am the first blind student in my school. It's been a rough road. My high school is small, about two hundred students, but I have talked to other people who are blind who went to smaller schools and loved it. I don't know what the deal is here.

One of the things that surprised me was how my friends reacted. I blame a portion of the way they reacted on the way my school handled it. They sent materials to the classes on "How to Treat a Blind Person." It said things like, "She's been in a traumatic accident. Don't hug her or make physical contact. If you are going to talk to her, talk to her personal aide."

I couldn't take being there anymore. I can't tell you how many teachers excluded me from group activities. They would say, "Courtney, you can just sit over here and listen." They didn't want to take the time to adapt it for me. Some schools bend over backwards, but not my school.

Now I'm finishing my high school degree at the local technical college. I love it at Tech. People talk to me and treat me like a normal person and actually include me. Next year, I'm going to Lake Shore Technical College about four hours from home. I'm going to major in court reporting and broadcast captioning.

All through my schooling I have gotten straight As, and one of my goals was to be valedictorian. I'm third in my class now, but it's going to be really tight all the way to the end. We are all within like .0000001 percent of each other. But this year, I've only been in my high school twice. I went to order graduation stuff and to get my yearbook pictures. I don't like being there.[3]

time, compared with 78 percent of those who do not have disabilities.[4]

On the bright side, the survey did show slow progress in the period since 1986, when NOD first started to collect information. That progress is being fueled by people like you, who stay in school and get the best education you can.

IDEA AND YOUR IEP

The Individuals with Disabilities Education Act (IDEA) is the federal law that drives most special education services in this country. IDEA requires that public schools provide students with disabilities a free, appropriate public education. Before this law existed, many young people with disabilities did not attend school because the buildings or class activities were not accessible. While things are different today, they are still not perfect, and there are still more changes to be made so that students with disabilities are given the same opportunities as their peers without disabilities. NOD believes that because of enforced legislation, accessible classrooms, the support of educators, and advances in assistive technology, students with disabilities have a fighting chance to close that gap.

Congress originally enacted IDEA in 1975, but it has been revised many times over the years, most recently in December 2004. According to the National Dissemination Center for Children with Disabilities (NICHCY), IDEA guides the means

Quinn Haberl works with his Braille/mobility instructor. Photo by Colleen Haberl.

states and school districts use to provide special education and related services to more than 6 million eligible students with disabilities.[5]

If you are a student with a disability, you probably already know that IDEA requires your public school to develop an individualized education program (IEP) for you each year. This is a written statement of how the school plans to meet your needs and states the services that the school district will provide for you.

By law, your IEP must include specific statements about you:

- **Your current level of achievement: How you are doing in school and how your disability affects your progress.**
- **Goals for the year: What the IEP team expects you to accomplish.**
- **Services: What services and other support you will receive, including assistive technology such as a communication device.**
- **Inclusion: How much of the school day you will spend being educated separately from students without disabilities and why.**
- **When and Where: When services and modifications will begin, how often they will be provided, where they will be provided, and how long they will last.**
- **Measuring Progress: How your progress toward the goals for the year will be measured and how often your parents will be informed.**
- **Transition Services: By the time you are sixteen, your IEP must include goals that address preparation for life after high school. These goals relate to further training and education, and employment and independent living skills.**

Many people come together to develop an IEP. Your team will include your parents, teachers, and other educators. Because your IEP is a legal document, some families bring a lawyer with them. Everyone on the team is devoted to creating the best plan possible, but the most important person on the team is you. You need to become your own best advocate.

KATY SANDBERG: TAKING CHARGE OF HER IEP

Katy, age twenty-two, is studying social work and journalism at the University of Wisconsin, Whitewater. She has cerebral palsy and controls her power wheelchair with a joystick.

I was lucky. I went to a high school with a really good special ed program. I had a one-on-one aide who took care of the physical stuff for me. Sometimes I liked my aides, sometimes I didn't, but it didn't matter because I had no choice. The first two years of high school went well.

Around my junior year I began having problems. When I started high school, I was determined to graduate in four years, but by my junior year I was getting stressed out by things like the ACT tests. I am not a really good standardized-test taker. The whole stress of college and being on my own and not knowing anybody—it made me really scared. I was so concerned about it that I decided I would need five years to graduate. That was a big problem. That meant I would not be able to walk in the ceremony with my own class. Instead I would have to graduate with my sister's class, and she is a year and a half younger than I am.

At my IEP meeting, my principal was there. I asked him if I could participate in the ceremony with my own friends. He said yes. So I got to go through the graduation ceremony with my class. When I got my diploma, for some stupid reason, my friends gave me a standing ovation.

That next year was a long one. I took a couple more classes at my high school, and then I took a semester at a local community college before coming here to University of Wisconsin, Whitewater. I didn't really want to stay at home that extra year, but those three classes at the community college helped me get used to the college experience.[6]

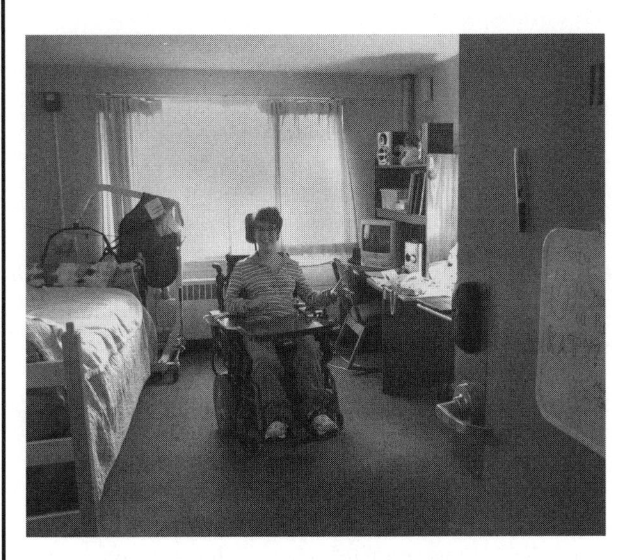

At home in Katy Sandberg's dorm room at University of Wisconsin, Whitewater. Photo by the author.

THE NATIONAL TECHNICAL INSTITUTE FOR THE DEAF (NTID)

The National Technical Institute for the Deaf (NTID) is the world's first and largest technological college for students who are deaf or hard of hearing. It is one of eight colleges of Rochester Institute of Technology (RIT) in Rochester, New York.

Here is the NTID/RIT story according to Karen Black, director of media relations at NTID:

> **After lobbying for years, the federal government decided a technical college was necessary for Deaf people because most Deaf people worked either on noisy printing presses or as teachers of Deaf children. The government put out a bid to colleges to host NTID, and RIT won it against many other national universities.**
>
> **The first class began in 1968 with twenty-seven students. Today, NTID has eleven hundred Deaf students who come to RIT to earn associate, bachelor's and master's degrees in more than two hundred programs. Deaf and hard-of-hearing students learn with various support services and the latest technology.**
>
> **The dean of the college is profoundly deaf, and there are about one hundred Deaf faculty and staff throughout campus. The dorms are deaf and hearing, as are the classrooms, sports fields, and social activities.**
>
> **Ninety percent of Deaf or hard-of-hearing people have hearing parents and siblings. In many cases, that person grows up in a hearing environment, and has attended mainstream schools as the only Deaf person in their school system. It can be a very isolated childhood. When they arrive at NTID, many are—for the first time in their lives—meeting others just like themselves. Because RIT is deaf (1,100 students) and hearing (14,400 students), it's exactly the environment they're used to and comfortable with. While other students who went to schools for the deaf also love it here because there is also a part of the hearing student body who embrace the Deaf culture and enjoy meeting others who were raised in that environment. Over and over, we've heard people say, "It's the best of both worlds at RIT because of the mainstreaming of deaf and hearing and the incredible access."**
>
> **Rochester, New York, has one of the world's largest Deaf communities, primarily because of NTID and the K–12 Rochester School for the Deaf. Many NTID/RIT graduates (we boast a 93 percent employment rate) stay in the area, work in the area, and raise their families. We now have their children as students too. Rochester is known as very Deaf friendly, and it's commonplace to see hearing workers at retailers, coffee shops, and restaurants signing to Deaf patrons. We have six Deaf doctors in town, and access to theater and movies is unprecedented. A Deaf docent works at the city's large art gallery, and the daily newspaper has a dedicated writer for stories related to hearing loss. People drive here from other states to see a current movie because open-captioned movies are just not as accessible in other places.[7]**

The most important thing for you to focus on is your transition plan. Look at the future and ask, How am I going to take care of myself? One way to begin is to get involved in qualifying for assistive services in the college or technical school of your choice.

"My first experience at a college campus I really freaked out," one teen in a wheelchair remembers. "I had a personal assistant. Then I found out she was lesbian, and to take care of me, you have to get pretty personal. When I said politely I didn't think that it was going to work out, she got really upset and started swearing at me. I definitely needed to build up my assertiveness before going away from home."

TECHNICAL COLLEGE

What comes after high school? If you are lucky enough to have a good idea of what you like to do and you want to get into the workforce as quickly as possible, you may want to continue your education at a technical college. These schools used to be called trade schools.

The long list of careers you can train for at a technical college includes fashion design, culinary arts, criminal justice, and dental hygiene. These are the kinds of jobs that directly meet a wide range of society's needs, and they can be very satisfying.

A technical education usually takes less time and generally costs less money than a four-year college degree. An average

Students with hearing impairment. Courtesy of the National Technical Institute for the Deaf at the Rochester Institute of Technology.

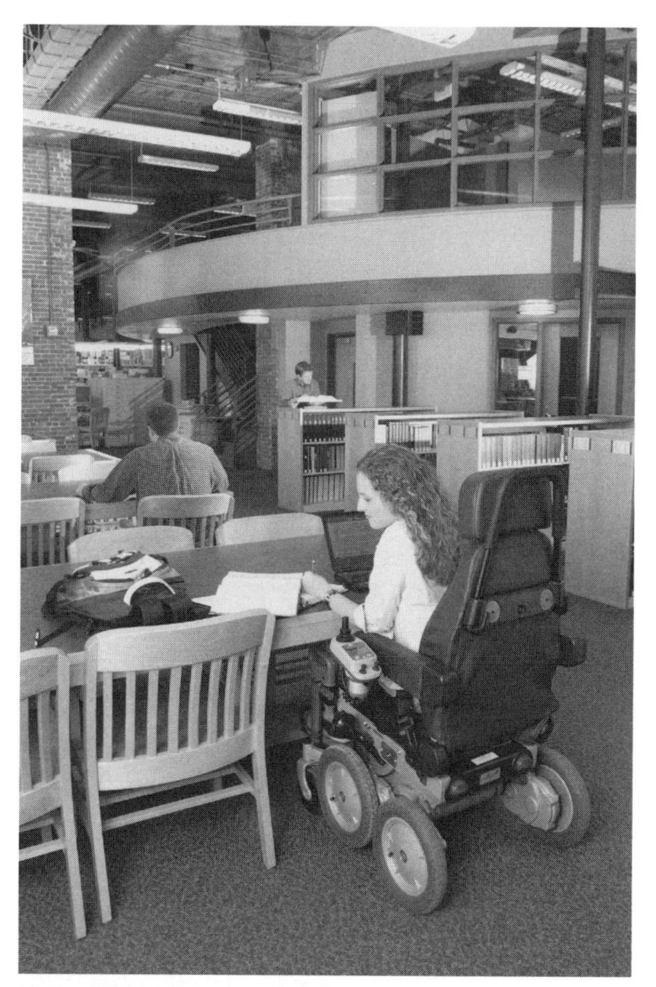

Megan Yekel uses her iBOT in the library. Courtesy of Independence Technology L.L.C.

program takes two years. Class schedules have to accommodate students who have busy work schedules or family responsibilities, so they tend to be more flexible than a traditional four-year undergraduate school.

Technical schools can be a great choice because they offer focused study and job training aimed at getting you out the door with specialized skills that will land you a job. Most technical schools base their reputation on how many of their graduates are employed, so they cultivate close ties with local employers and will be able to offer you genuine job leads.

However, your education at a technical school may not be as well rounded as that offered at a four-year college. If you decide you want to be a dentist instead of a dental hygienist, you will have to go back to school and complete a bachelor's degree.

COLLEGE

You've decided to go to college. It's a big decision. Now you have to make an even bigger one. Picking your college is one of the major stresses of being a high school senior, but if you have a disability, you'd better start stressing as a junior. Just like everyone else, you need to weigh the academic considerations and the social atmosphere, but you also need to find out how well you will be able to fit into that particular campus community. You want to know that every aspect of your major and related studies will be available to you. Then you need to ask about other facets of campus life. Where will you live? Are there adaptive sports? You must explore personal assistance services, the accessibility of the classrooms, and the curricula. It is worth it to find the right fit for you.

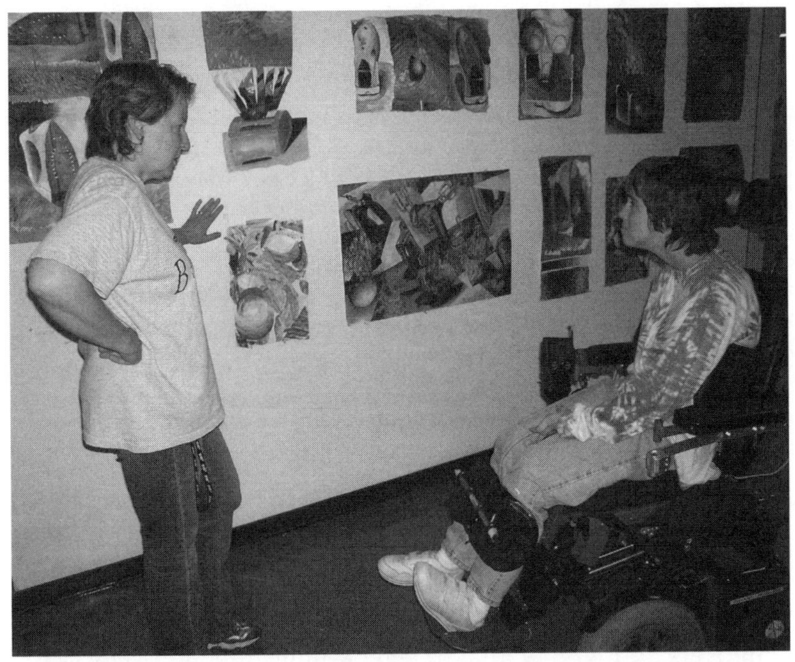

Statia Wilson discusses painting techniques with her art professor, Sam Norgard, at University of Wisconsin, Whitewater. Photo by the author.

ANGELA KUEMMEL: GOING FAR FROM HOME WAS A HARD DECISION

Twenty-three-year-old Angela Kuemmel is pursuing a Ph.D. degree in psychological studies. A diving accident paralyzed her from the chest down at age fifteen.

I wanted to be a doctor. I wanted to work with people who had spinal cord injuries. I started looking at schools that had strong pre-med programs. I applied to nine or ten schools. I was invited to St. Louis University for a full scholarship. I loved it. It was accessible, and the people were great. I was accepted into their medical scholars program, but my parents didn't want me going so far away. It was a very hard decision.

My mom gave me really good advice. We were crying in the kitchen. She said, "Angela, this is really scary for me, too. But I can see you would really like to be at St. Louis. If you go and you don't like it, you can always come back, but if you don't try it, you'll never know."

The first semester was really tough. I think your first semester of college is hard regardless of where you go—disability or no disability. I have a really supportive family that I'm really close to. It was hard to be far from home and living on my own. I ended up meeting great people, and it all worked out.

I was the first person in a wheelchair to live in a dorm there. They put in a roll-in shower, and I lived in the room by myself. I needed help with laundry and cleaning, but I'm independent in all my self-care.

Hiring people to help you is a scary big deal. Especially when you are far from home and Mom and Dad can't save you. I found an aide by advertising through the occupational therapy and physical therapy students. This is a great strategy—all the fields for people who are going to work with people with disabilities. A nursing or special education student would also be good. It's good for them.

I switched to psychology my sophomore year, and I've never regretted it. Now I'm in a doctoral program in Nova Southeastern University at Fort Lauderdale, Florida. Again, it's really far away. I never intended to go so far as I ended up. I applied to fourteen schools. I got invited down for an interview, went there, and was so impressed. I was accepted into their health psychology concentration. The Miami Project is the largest spinal cord research center in the country.

I have three more years of school, then a one-year internship. I'm hoping that my having a spinal cord injury is going to make me more marketable. I have wanted to work with people with spinal cord injury since I was fifteen and had my injury. When you have the experience, you have better understanding than those who haven't been through it.[8]

When you finally arrive on campus you will find yourself in a very different world than high school. The hall monitors and parental teachers are gone. You are going to have to take more responsibility for yourself. Most students find they have to pick up the pace to keep up with classes when they make the leap from high school to college. As a student with a disability, you need to think very carefully about the strategies you will use to handle the increased academic competition in a

LAURA GLOWACKI: BE YOUR OWN ADVOCATE

Laura, age nineteen, has been blind since birth. She left public high school to attend her state's school for the visually impaired. Now she is attending college.

I switched from public school to the Illinois School for the Visually Impaired when I was a sophomore in high school. In public school, I was always the smart kid in class. Other kids wanted me in their school groups, but after school, they didn't ask me to do anything. I had success in public school. I got the acclaim and support, but I wanted social and extracurricular activities.

At ISVI I felt very accepted, but it did take getting used to. There were a lot of rules, and I had to remember the rules, and I had to learn the campus—how to walk between various buildings. The classrooms were great, and they all had braillers in them. A Perkins Brailler is a big, clunky, metal typewriter-looking thing with only eight keys. We did a lot of our schoolwork on them. We also had screen reader software to make the computer talk to us already loaded onto the computers.

I will say public school was great for teaching me how to be my own advocate. The advocacy thing is horribly important, and my teachers worked on it. By fourth grade, they had me call the Library of Congress and order my own textbooks in Braille for the next year. I got to understand how the process works. I learned phone skills and people skills. In public school, I had to go to my teachers and tell them what accommodations I would need in the classroom. Being able to speak for yourself is so important. I see so many people whose parents want to do everything for them, and it drives me nuts. They can't be dependent on their parents forever. There is just no way.

It was a big adjustment from ISVI back to public school when I came to college. At first I was miserable. My biggest challenge was getting around campus. Due to a couple of minor screw-ups, there was no orientation mobility instructor to show me around the first few days. I had been given one lesson on the buildings in the summer, but I didn't remember how to get between buildings. I have a good memory, but not that good. I just wandered around trying to get to class. Sometimes I got lucky, but if I had to go to a place I wasn't used to, it totally freaked me out. Now my orientation mobility instructor has shown me around. He will work on the bus system with me too. I don't have to use buses now, but I will eventually.

(*continued*)

LAURA GLOWACKI: BE YOUR OWN ADVOCATE (*continued*)

My academic classes are going well. I have music theory, English, and music appreciation. I take notes on a PAC Mate Braille writer. I write my papers on my computer and e-mail them to my professors. My teachers take my tests over to the disability support office, and they put it in Braille. I go to the office when the rest of the class is taking the test, and they give it to me in Braille. I type out my answers, and they get it back to the professor. If I have to read anything, I can get in on tape or in text format on the computer.

My challenge is that I'm a music major, and I can't read music. I didn't start early enough. Braille music is really hard to read. Right now in concert choir, I learn the music by ear. The conductor seated me next to a singer who is very loud and very good.

I'm probably going to end up spending five years to finish college. I'll get a degree in music therapy. I haven't done any field experience yet, but I think I want to work with kids with developmental disabilities or troubled teens. They are both pretty tough groups to work with, and I may end up changing my mind, but I'm drawn to those kids. I had horrible self-esteem when I was twelve to fourteen and don't want anyone to have to go through that. I can't save the world, obviously. But I want to help teens—they need plenty of help.[9]

world where teachers and parents are no longer making decisions for you. You will have to build your own network of support.

"To qualify for services, you need to be substantially limited in one or more major life activity," explains Deb Claire, accommodations specialist at the McBurney Disability Resource Center of the University of Wisconsin, Madison. "It can be very difficult to determine who is disabled enough to receive extra services, but once it is determined, we have a legal obligation to serve you and put you on an even playing field. It's not a guarantee of success but a fair shot. It's all about access."[10]

"As a high school student, it's best if you have a really good idea about what you need and put it down in advance when you are considering a college," says Annie Robertson,

REBECCA WYLIE: CREATING A COLLEGE EXPERIENCE

Rebecca graduated from high school in the top ten of her class and was awarded the John F. Kennedy Medal of Honor. She is a graphic design major at the University of Missouri, and she is quadriplegic. She wasn't born with a disability. At the end of first grade she came down with transverse myelitis. She had no symptoms other than being really tired. When she woke up from a nap, her arms were tingly. Within an hour, she couldn't move her arms, then her legs, and then her breathing became very rapid. Her spinal cord had become so swollen that no messages were getting through, and when the swelling went down, there was so much scar tissue left that messages still couldn't get through.

I really like college at the University of Missouri. It's way different than high school. I feel so much more independent. When I was in high school, they treated me like a child. Here they treat me like an adult. I have a lot more freedom now.

My family lives in Illinois, and I considered the University of Illinois because it is called the number one campus for accessibility. But their wheelchair housing is off campus, and they put everyone in wheelchairs in one dorm. I think that is segregation. I didn't want to go live with just people in wheelchairs. I want to be with regular students too.

I'm living in a regular dorm. I had to hire four people to help me. I need help with everything, including feeding. The university has nursing, physical, and occupational therapy programs, so I contacted the individual departments and asked them to put up flyers and tell professors to let their students know about the jobs. The disability services office also compiled a list of people who were interested. Now I have a lot of backup if someone is going home for the weekend. Sometimes all four of them can't be here. Labor Day weekend, they all went home.

I've heard horror stories that a lot of people don't realize being a helper is a serious job. You can't just blow somebody off and not come at 6:30 in the morning to get someone up. Because I'm eight hours from home, it's not like my parents can come take care of me if the people I've hired don't. If a crisis comes up, I'll have to hire a full-time nurse to get me up and put me to bed at night. But the more people I get interested in being backup, the less that will come up.

(***continued***)

REBECCA WYLIE:
CREATING A COLLEGE EXPERIENCE (*continued*)

My disability doesn't hurt my schoolwork. I'm in the honors college. I'm taking fifteen credits, which is the average, and I have no problem. I type my own papers with a mouth stick. I have voice-activated software, and I use that too. Next semester I'm taking art classes. I'll do that with my mouth stick.

I don't have an aide in class. I do get a volunteer note taker. The other work that I do is reading. I can't hold a book, so the university buys an extra set of my textbooks, cuts them open and scans each page, then posts them on the Internet for me. I type in a password, and there are my books. I also use books on tape.

I'm taking English, a writing course, American history, psychology, and geology. That's a lab science. Because I can't use my arms, I've hired another student as my lab assistant. I tell her what to do, and she acts as my hands.

I honestly don't think of myself as disabled because, basically, I can do anything any other college student can do. I've got a joystick and enough hand movement in my left hand to operate my wheelchair. I can dial the phone. I can operate the computer. My dorm has an automatic door that I can open without a key.

There are four other people in wheelchairs on my floor. One girl has had a lot of trouble finding people to work for her. Her mom has been living with her all last year and this year. I think they may not be trying hard enough. I wouldn't like that at all. My parents told me they weren't going to go to college with me, and I didn't want them to. It was a long process to find people to help me, but it's way better than having my parents here.

I chose to go far away because I want the normal college experience. I want normal classes and atmosphere and friends.[11]

also an accommodations specialist at the McBurney Disability Resource Center. "That gives the college time to coordinate—to make a plan and a budget. That really helps the school.

"When you come into college from high school, you are used to intensive support—teachers, special ed counselors, parents. Once a student is eighteen, we cannot contact his or her parents without the student's consent. It's a shock to some people. But if they are going to succeed, they need to become

MICHELLE SUZANNE MALONEY: BETWEEN HEARING AND DEAF WORLDS

Twenty-three-year-old Michelle is a rehabilitation psychology graduate student. Her goal is to be a rehabilitation counselor in a university setting.

From any disability perspective, self-advocacy is really important. Especially going from high school to college, you can't depend on your parents. You have to stand up to get what you need. I had to learn how to explain my disability to others and be comfortable with that.

I am studying rehabilitation psychology. I always wanted to help people. I have severe hearing loss in my right ear and moderate loss in my left ear. Why I do is a mystery. I was diagnosed when I was two years old. My vocabulary level is lower than the average person my age because I started out two years without hearing. They say it is common for people with hearing loss to have lower vocabulary levels. That was an issue for me when I applied to grad school. When you take the Graduate Record Exams, you have to get a certain score on the verbal and the math sections. My verbal score was low in relationship to my grade point average. I asked my college adviser to write a letter explaining my vocabulary.

I'm not completely deaf, and it can be hard being in between. Some people who are totally deaf are very strong into the Deaf culture. They consider they have their own culture. They have their own language—American Sign Language—and their own communities. They don't see themselves as disabled.

When I was in elementary school, I used an FM system, which was very stigmatizing. It was a brown box with a cord that went to your ears. The teacher wore a microphone, so what the teacher said went straight to your ears. It was supposed to be better than a hearing aid, but I didn't like it because it was very apparent that I was hard of hearing. The thing was frustrating in a group project. I couldn't hear what people were saying unless they passed the microphone around. In sixth grade, I got rebellious and said I wouldn't wear it any more.

I've always considered myself part of the hearing world, but right now I'm having a hard time with two of my three classes. One professor has an accent, and it is hard to understand him. He suggested that I get an interpreter or a stenographer who can do real-time captioning. But I was hesitant because that draws a lot of attention, and I've never felt deaf enough to need that. Plus, I might be taking that service away from someone who might need it more. When I finally decided that I really needed to take the service, then I had to make an appointment with my adaptive counselor. By the time I finally get the services approved, the semester will be almost over.[12]

very responsible. We empower students to use accommodations while they are here because after they graduate, they are on their own.

"Our students are in charge of their own toolbox, and the accommodations are the tools to pursue their path. We can make accommodations, but that won't alter the program requirements. They are going to be responsible for the same type of work that everyone else is.

GALLAUDET UNIVERSITY: A WIDE RANGE OF PROGRAMS FOR DEAF AND HARD-OF-HEARING PEOPLE

In its report "America's Best Colleges 2006," *U.S. News & World Report* designated Gallaudet University number one in the magazine's "Best Value: Universities—Master's" category for four-year liberal arts colleges and universities in the northern region. In addition, Gallaudet University ranks among the top twenty-five overall in its region.

Gallaudet University in Washington, D.C., provides a wide range of programs for Deaf and hard-of-hearing people from around the world. The university offers undergraduate, graduate, and doctoral degrees.

Deaf and hard-of-hearing undergraduate students can choose from more than thirty majors. They also have the option of designing their own majors by selecting classes from a variety of departments at Gallaudet or taking courses offered at eleven other institutions of higher learning that are members of the Consortium of Universities of the Washington Metropolitan Area.

Beginning in 2005, a two- to three-year pilot program was initiated to admit a small number of hearing undergraduate students—no more than 2 percent of the entering class. Graduate programs are open to Deaf, hard-of-hearing, and hearing students.

U.S. News & World Report examines more than 500 universities in the "Universities—Master's" category annually. In 2005, 2006, and 2007, Gallaudet made the "Best Value" list. The formula used for best value considers a school's academic quality, as indicated by its *U.S. News* ranking, and the net cost of attendance for a student who receives the average level of need-based financial aid. The higher the quality of the program and the lower the cost, the better the deal.

Gallaudet has a strong commitment to using technology as a means of enhancing its academic programs. Many on-campus courses have a heavy emphasis on the Internet and multimedia technologies, and the number of courses offered completely online for local and remote students is growing rapidly.

"For most people college is your first chance to live independently. The college setting is the best setting to explore your needs—to figure out what works and what doesn't. It's a safe place to explore."[13]

RESOURCES

College Funding Strategies for Students with Disabilities. These valuable guidelines have been prepared by the University of Washington. www.washington.edu/doit/Brochures/Academics/financial-aid.html

Making Accommodations. Learn about the legal world of students with disabilities. www.ahead.org/resources/articles.htm

New Mobility Magazine has a very comprehensive article on disability-friendly colleges. www.newmobility.com/review_article.cfm?id=122&action=browse

Preparing for College. This online tutorial includes just about everything you will need to know. Visit it early and often. www.washington.edu/doit/Brochures/Academics/cprep.html

NOTES

1. Webpage created as part of an exhibition and commemoration of the life and work of César E. Cháves by UCLA, clnet.ucla.edu/research/chavez (November 17, 2006) and webpage of quotations, thinkexist.com/quotes/like/we_cannot_seek_achievement_for_ourselves_and/202003/2.html (November 17, 2006).
2. Jessie Martin, interview with author, April 12, 2005.
3. Courtney Glodowski, interview with author, October 11, 2005.
4. National Organization on Disability, "Landmark Disability Survey Finds Pervasive Disadvantages," June 25, 2004, www.nod.org/index.cfm?fuseaction=page.viewPage&pageID=1430&nodeID=1&FeatureID=1422&redirected=1&CFID=5338505&CFTOKEN=2857954 (October 17, 2005).
5. National Dissemination Center for Children with Disabilities, "IDEA," www.nichcy.org/idea.htm (July 13, 2005).
6. Katy Sandberg, interview with author, September 22, 2005.

7. Karen Black, e-mail, October 17, 2005.
8. Angela Kuemmel, interview with author, September 28, 2005.
9. Laura Glowacki, interview with author, September 1, 2005.
10. Deb Claire, interview with author, March 31, 2005.
11. Rebecca Wylie, interview with author, October 17, 2003.
12. Michelle Suzanne Maloney, interview with author, October 4, 2005.
13. Annie Robertson, interview with author, March 25, 2005.

2 Tools and Technology

From microwaves to cell phones to PalmPilots, technology is exploding and is enhancing many lives. If you have a disability, these technical options can spell increased independence. Developments in computer software, materials science, and miniaturization are racing forward quickly. Be sure to check out the resources listed at the end of this chapter to find more information about the most current products.

"My computer is my life. When it breaks down it's pretty rough. But I have some great friends to help me out."

—Statia Wilson, 22, college art major with cerebral palsy[1]

Assistive technology is any tool, gadget, or piece of equipment that you use to do a task that you otherwise couldn't do, or something that helps you do things more easily, more quickly, or better. Technology ranges from something as simple as a pencil grip to an electronic Braille notepad, from strobe light smoke detectors to talking wristwatches. This chapter will explore some of the technology that can help you get through the day. Some are time tested and others are fresh from the drawing board.

"We at independent living centers assert that having a disability is natural," says Michael Hineberg of IndependenceFirst. "Disability does not make someone better or worse, just different, and we look for the tools we need to do the job. You remember things—I write them down. You take the stairs—I take the elevator. One person performs all his or her personal cares independently—another person has a helper. If you found yourself on the side of a mountain cliff without bolts or belays, you would have a disability. No two people are the same. Find the right tools, and you can do it."[2]

ADAPTIVE TELEPHONES

Depending on the extent of an individual's hearing loss, amplification devices can give access to telephones. They have features like tone control or variable ring sounds, flashing lights, and large dial buttons (some people with hearing loss may also have vision loss), or an audio jack to connect to an additional listening device. For people with visual or mobility impairment, phones can be voice activated and can feature a talking form of caller ID.

The Ameritech Special Needs Center, facilitated by HITEC Group International, provides information about communication equipment designed to assist people who are deaf, hard of hearing, visually impaired, speech impaired, or who have limited mobility. The center's job is to match consumers with appropriate devices. Check out HITEC's website at www.hitec.com.

ALTERNATE KEYBOARDS

For most of us, the keyboard is truly the key to using a computer. Keyboards can vary in size, layout, and complexity to suit individual needs. Programmable keyboards are configured so that specific letters, numbers, words, or phrases can be entered by pressing custom keys. Others can be larger, making it easier to hit the right keys. Miniature ones allow individuals with a small range of motion to access all the keys. Chording keyboards have fewer keys, and you enter text by pressing combinations of keys at once. Some keyboards are images on the computer screen where keys can be selected by mouse, touch screen, or other electronic pointing devices.

AMERICAN SIGN LANGUAGE

According to the National Institute on Deafness and Other Communication Disorders, American Sign Language, or ASL, is a language completely separate from English. It is said to be the fourth most commonly used language in the United States.

Everyone is familiar with it, but what is it exactly? Whereas spoken languages are based on sounds and tone of voice, ASL is a complete and complex language made up of hand signs, facial expressions, and body posture. English speakers often ask a question by raising their voice at the end of a sentence. ASL users raise their eyebrows and widen their eyes.

Like spoken language, no one form of sign language is universal. Different countries use different signs. Signs vary by region just as accents do in spoken language. And although it is used in the United States, ASL has its own rules of grammar, punctuation, and sentence order.

Learning American Sign Language is like studying any other language. It takes years of dedicated study to become fluent. Finger spelling is a part of communicating with sign language and is easier to learn. It can provide a stopgap form of communication between the Deaf and the hearing.

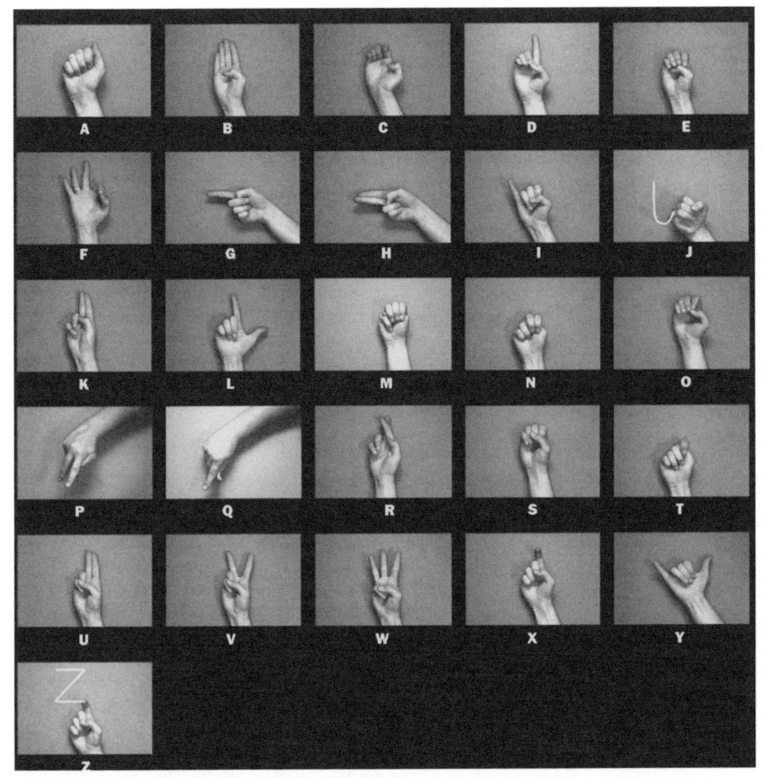

American Sign Language finger spelling alphabet. Courtesy of iStockphoto.

ARTIFICIAL ARMS AND LEGS, OR PROSTHETICS

According to the National Limb Loss Information Center, about one out of every two hundred people in the United States has had a limb amputated. The figures for 1996 estimated 1.2 million persons were living with limb loss.[3] Many of these people get around and manage their lives with the use of artificial arms and legs, feet and hands called prosthetics. Compared to one hundred or even twenty years ago, artificial limbs are amazing. Advances in material can provide a more lifelike look and feel, and advances in joint controls, many of which are controlled by microprocessors, give more lifelike action.

Legs

Two examples of artificial leg technology are the Otto Bock C-Leg knee and the Iceland-based Ossur Rheo Knee. They represent a quantum leap in joint technology, using microprocessors to control the knee's hydraulic function, automatically fine-tuning itself from fifty to one hundred times a second, anticipating what the wearer is doing and accommodating every change in real time. Ossur says its knee is the first in a new generation of microprocessor-controlled swing and stance knee systems that incorporate artificial intelligence, giving the system the ability to learn how the user walks.[4]

Arms and Hands

Artificial arms and hands are constantly improving. Many users have different devices that they exchange depending on what they want to do. There are many choices. Some artificial hands primarily aim to look natural, and a modern silicone hand can come close. According to Motion Control, an artificial arm maker, many amputees can use a body-powered hook prosthesis for some activities, like rugged hobbies such as woodworking and sports, and an electric hand for working in public. There is a combination electric and body-powered

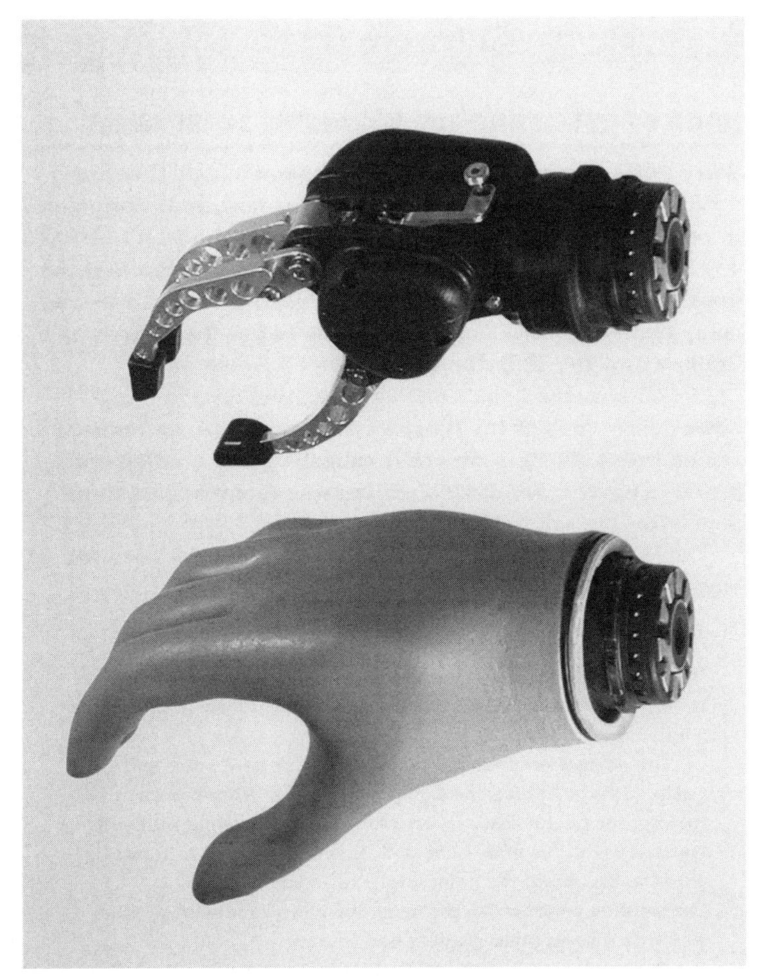

Prosthetic hands. Courtesy of Motion Control.

prosthesis called a hybrid. Such a prosthesis might have a body-powered elbow and an electric hand. The newest electric hands, wrists, and elbows operate by using muscle signals from the remnant limb and may provide the most natural function of all.[5]

BRAILLE

"Before my accident I didn't even know Braille existed," says Courtney Glodowski. "Now it is my life."[6]

Braille is a system that uses different arrangements of dots to make up letters of the alphabet, numbers, and punctuation

HARRY POTTER AND THE WIZARDRY OF BRAILLE

Harry Potter fanatics swarm bookstores at midnight before each new volume appears. They want to know what Harry has to endure next, and they want to know *now*. You won't find any Braille readers in those midnight lines. When the first five books in the series were released, Braille readers had to wait many torturous weeks or even months to get their hands on a Braille copy. The sixth time, they didn't have to wait.

Scholastic, the book's publisher, agreed to give a top-secret early copy of the Harry Potter text to the National Braille Press (NBP), a nonprofit publishing and printing house based in Boston. The Braille edition was released just three days after the printed book hit the shelves.

Tanya Holton, vice president of development at the NBP, says:

> We were thrilled. We had an agreement with Scholastic to get the text in advance in a secure location. We were able to get it out in seventeen days. We did a lot of overtime to make this work.
>
> The normal process for taking a mainstream book and putting it into Braille can take up to a year. We are always looking for books that mainstream kids are reading that will translate well for blind kids. J. K. Rowling creates a wonderful world in the mind. It's completely up to the reader's imagination to draw the pictures. We knew immediately that this was a book blind readers had to have.
>
> As we started to put the first Harry Potter book through our process, the hype began. We ramped up the schedule, but it still took about seven months to get the book into Braille. Two years later, when the next book came out, we were a little ahead of the game. The day it came out, we started processing it.
>
> Finally with the sixth book in the series, Braille readers had almost instant access. NBP also produces the book in electronic refreshable Braille. It's so liberating for kids and adults alike to have Braille at their fingertips in a much more portable format. We have sold more Harry Potter books than any other publication. It flies off the shelf.
>
> We are trying to offer equality. Really Harry Potter is an example of inclusion. It's all about allowing blind readers to have a mainstream experience of a cultural phenomenon. As one reader said, "We had to wait two years for the next book. That's hard enough. Why should we have to wait longer?" Equal access to information is what we aim for.[7]

HARRY POTTER AND THE WIZARDRY OF BRAILLE (*continued*)

The NBP's version of *Harry Potter and the Half-Blood Prince* runs approximately one thousand Braille pages. It is packaged in eight volumes standing more than a foot high and weighs about eleven pounds. To produce the Braille version costs about $62 per book, approximately three times as much as Scholastic's print version. However, NBP policy is to charge blind readers the same prices paid by sighted readers. Donations to the NBP make up the difference.

The first five books in the Harry Potter series have sold more briskly in hard-copy, paper Braille than in the electronic versions. One reason is that many blind readers lack access to the technology needed to read electronic Braille. A single Braille copy of any Harry Potter book will be read by many people because blind readers often share or borrow copies of favorite books. The Library of Congress also runs Braille lending libraries in each state.

Copies of *Harry Potter and the Goblet of Fire* printed in Braille. Courtesy of the National Braille Press.

marks. The basic symbol is called a cell. It is made up of six dots arranged in a rectangle, three dots high and two across. Experienced readers can read Braille at speeds of up to four hundred words a minute.

Braille was first developed in about 1820 by Louis Braille in France. Louis created the system before he was eighteen by modifying a system of night writing that was used on ships. Louis was blinded by an accident that resulted in an eye infection when he was three. He attended a school for the blind, where he and his friends found that reading and writing dots was much faster than reading raised print, which could not be written by hand at all. His system is now recognized as the most important single development in giving blind students access to education, but it took more than a century for Braille to be universally accepted.

Even today, many people don't realize how effective Braille is. According to the National Braille Press, forty-nine thousand people under the age of twenty-two in the United States are legally blind. Only 9 percent read Braille.

Some people think that in an age of recorded books and computerized voice readers that Braille is not as important, but Mike Tindell of the National Federation of the Blind disagrees. "We do have computers today with speech," he says. "I use them, but it is one thing to be able to hear something and a whole different story to be able to read and comprehend it. It would be as if all you learned came from the radio and TV, but you never saw anything in print. Braille is the only way we have of physically reading a book or anything else we want or need to read. For blind people to be literate, they need to know Braille."[8]

COCHLEAR IMPLANT

The cochlear implant is a tiny, complex electronic device that can help provide a sense of sound to a person who is profoundly deaf or severely hard of hearing. It is surgically placed under the skin behind the ear.

According to the National Institutes of Health, in a normal ear, sounds transmitted through the air cause the eardrum, then the middle ear bones, and finally the cochlea to vibrate. The vibrations in the cochlea are converted to electrical signals that travel along the auditory nerve to the brain.

Most cochlear implants have several components. Sound is picked up by a microphone worn near the ear. A speech processor worn on the body analyzes the sound and converts it to electrical signals. These are transmitted to a surgically implanted receiver behind the ear. This receiver sends the signal through a wire into the inner ear and on to the brain.

Surgery to insert a cochlear implant must take place with the patient fully asleep. A drill opens the bone behind the ear so the internal part of the implant can be inserted in a "well" created behind the ear. The electrode array is then passed into the inner ear.

A cochlear implant cannot restore or create normal hearing. Instead it provides a sense of sound. After the cochlear implant is in place, the patient must undertake a

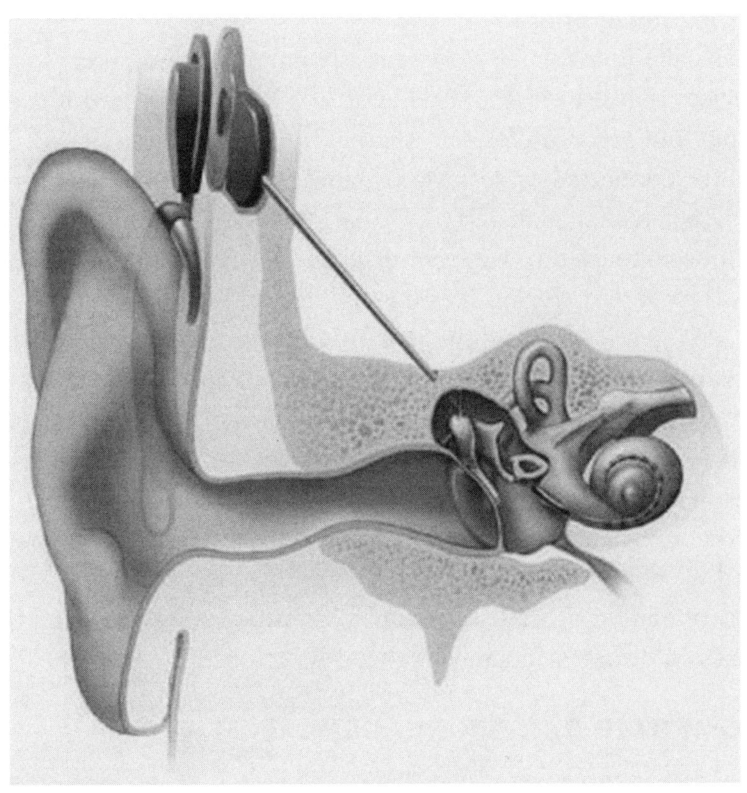

Anatomy of a cochlear implant. Courtesy of the National Institute on Deafness and Other Communication Disorders.

significant amount of learning so the brain can make sense of its input.

One of the most advanced cochlear implant devices is the HiResolution Bionic Ear System. You can learn more at www.engadget.com/2006/09/28/harmony-hiresolution-bionic-ear-system-gets-fda-nod.

REFRESHABLE BRAILLE DISPLAY AND BRAILLE NOTE TAKERS

Conventional Braille is embossed onto paper, but refreshable Braille displays provide computer access to people who are visually impaired when they don't want a synthesizer reading out loud. A mechanical display provides tactile output of the information on the computer screen by lifting tiny, rounded plastic or metal pins along a pad to form Braille characters. After the line is read, the display can be "refreshed" to read the next line. It also gives precise information about screen formatting in Braille.

Braille note takers are essentially handheld computer devices that use either a Braille or QWERTY keyboard for input and voice and/or refreshable Braille for output. They can be connected to desktop or laptop computers so that files may be created, transferred, or backed up. Some note takers can be connected to external disk drives (for an additional cost) to permit storing files on a disk.

PAC Mate by Freedom Scientific is basically an accessible pocket PC that combines the function to read the screen out loud and to produce it in refreshable Braille. "We have made a mainstream system for handheld devices accessible," says Justin Fegel, marketing and communications specialist at Freedom Scientific. "We can access a clock, a calendar, e-mail, and we have also added other programs to expand its functionality. We have our own word processor and calculator that can do scientific and financial functions."[9]

COMPUTER SCREEN READER

The computer screen reader is software that can read out loud or produce in Braille what appears on a computer's monitor.

An example of a powerful and popular screen reader is JAWS, created by Freedom Scientific.[10] It is designed to work with Windows programs and can translate any text that appears on the screen into synthetic speech or Braille. JAWS can work with a variety of speech synthesizers, which have a number of voices and allow the user to customize them. The user can set the pitch and the speed, so you can set one voice for messages and a different voice for a cursor, for example.

"There are people who use screen readers really quickly. They have the reader cranked up to several hundred words a minute," says Fegel. "You can read Braille and process it faster than you can process speech. You can see how things are spelled and written out, and it's easier to flip the electronically refreshable Braille display back to review."[11]

ELECTRONIC PRINT MAGNIFIER

An electronic print magnifier is software, such as MAGic by Freedom Scientific, blows up the text that you see on your computer screen. The user just boots up the computer, and the

Enlarged computer print. Courtesy of Northcentral Technical College, Wausau, Wisconsin.

text is automatically enlarged. It also allows the user to place a book or other printed matter on the scanner and read it at a larger print size on the computer screen.

OPTICAL CHARACTER RECOGNITION AND READING SOFTWARE AND DEVICES

Optical character recognition works with a speech synthesizer to convert printed documents into electronic text, then read it out loud so the user can listen to a printed page. The software can include a search feature, a thesaurus, a dictionary, a spell checker, and a talking calculator. Documents can be e-mailed, downloaded, and burned to CDs.

With products like Freedom Scientific's OpenBook software, you can listen to, scan, and read mail, school handouts, books, magazines, and CD covers. You can save homework and program a calendar to let you know when it is due. The same company also makes SARA, which stands for scanning and reading appliance. Users can save documents in it or burn them to a CD. It has twenty different languages, so it can read your Spanish homework as well.

"The latest scanners are getting more and more intelligent," says Fegel. "There is a margin of error. The synthesizer tries its best to read everything, but they do get some words wrong. Names especially can be very individual. A lot of screen readers get around that by building in a dictionary. If you have a word the reader is speaking incorrectly, you can add it to the dictionary and instruct the reader how to pronounce it."[12]

PC-TO-PC CALLS

Voice chat is used by people like seventeen-year-old Karrie Kinstetter, who has been blind since birth. Yahoo! says about its Messenger with Voice, "[J]ust plug a headset into your computer and click the Call button. If you're offline or away from the computer, your friends can leave you a voicemail. You can assign special ringtones to different contacts on your messenger list, so you'll know who is calling."[13]

ANNIE CONNOR: AN ARSENAL OF ASSISTIVE TECHNOLOGY

Annie Connor was a National Merit Scholar in high school. Now a University of Wisconsin, Madison student, she is aiming to be a special education teacher.

I am taking seventeen credits. I am an academic co-coordinator for our dorm hall association, and I have a part-time job. It makes for a busy Annie. I have always loved to be busy. Before I got sick, I loved gymnastics, and I was on a swim team. I love my classes, and I love seeing my friends. How can I not be active?

Perhaps a better question is how *can* she be active? Annie has complex regional pain syndrome. CRPS is pain that occurs after an injury to an arm or a leg. The cause of the syndrome is not known. The pain is often described as a burning sensation.

I got it when I was eleven. I sprained my ankle, and it never healed right. It's one of the most painful diseases. Bone pain. Joint pain. Muscle pain. It's gotten worse over time. Now I can't use my right side. My right leg is in a cast. I need crutches or a walker to get around. I try to work around it, but sometimes I can't.

Annie has an arsenal of assistive technology she has gathered together to keep up the pace she sets for herself.

I wear a brace when I am writing. I use Dragon 8 NaturallySpeaking to write my assignments. Dragon is amazing. I can talk, and it will type for me. I can tell the computer "scratch that," or "edit that" or I can tell it to "spell that," and verbally spell out a word. I also use a Kensington track ball mouse. It's the size of a billiard ball with buttons on both sides. I just put my palm on it.

I use a headset with my phone to save my hands. I have an ergonomically correct chair, and it helps me sit up right when I'm having a bad day.

When I play cards with my friends, I have a card-holding device. I use an adapted cutting board to hold a piece of bread still, and it has spikes to hold fruit. I use a big-grip knife and a pizza cutter. All ergonomic grips help. I have a pot stabilizer so I can stir a pot on the stove, and last but not least, I have elastic laces in my shoes that are curlicues so you can just pull them. They sell them in rehab magazines now. They were a fad when I was in sixth grade.

For getting around, I have a key holder that holds up to three keys and it lets me turn the key with my shoulder. I snap my keys to my pack with carabineer clips. I have an armrest platform on my walker so I can take the pressure through my elbows and forearms instead of my wrist, which doesn't bend. I can put spikes on my crutches when it's icy, but I try to use my walker on ice. I'm not supposed to do stairs at all. When I have to use stairs, I have to crawl.

My friends say I'm strong, but sometimes I don't feel so strong. Sometimes I just want to walk down to the student union with my friends, but I can't, and that's hard. It hurts to have to go bed when friends are ready to go out. I am a very independent person. I have been for a long time. It's not easy for me to ask for help, but I have learned that sometimes I have to, and in the process I have learned a lot about my good friends, and who they are. People who will do things like go get my dinner when I can't get out of bed regardless of how much homework they have. I have such good friends. I am very, very lucky.[14]

SERVICE DOGS

People have been using dogs for assistance since before recorded history. Service dogs can do many tasks. We are most familiar with guide dogs that are trained to help blind or visually impaired people. They navigate their owners through traffic, stairs, and sidewalks and keep them out of harm's way.

Hearing dogs are trained to alert their Deaf owners to sounds their owner needs to know about, like doorbells, phones, smoke alarms, crying babies, and microwave beeps. They are trained to approach their owners and then return to the source of the sound. Hearing dogs have the same access privileges as guide dogs and are permitted in all public and private facilities.

Mobility assist dogs may pull their owners' wheelchairs, carry things in a backpack, pick up things their owners drop, open and close doors, and even help their owners dress.

TTY OR TEXT TELEPHONE

The TTY device lets people who are deaf, hard of hearing, or speech impaired use the telephone to communicate by allowing them to type messages instead of talking and listening.

Many organizations have a separate phone number marked TTY in their contact information, because a TTY is required on both phones to converse. If you don't have a TTY, you can still call a person who is deaf, hard of hearing, or speech impaired by using the telecommunications relay service (TRS). With TRS, a communications assistant (CA) types whatever you say so that the person you are calling can read your words on his or her TTY display. He or she types back a response, which the CA reads aloud for you to hear over the phone. A CA's responsibility is to relay the conversation exactly as it is received. All relay calls are confidential.

Because the Americans with Disabilities Act (ADA) of 1990 requires all telephone companies in the United States to provide telecommunications relay services, toll-free TRS services are available twenty-four hours a day, 365 days a

A BOY AND HIS DOG

As a blind orphan in India who could barely swallow, Quinn Haberl was on his way to becoming a decimal point in a tragic statistic. When he arrived in the United States at twenty-one months of age, the doctors said his organs were starting to shut down, but he defied their expectations and began to gain weight. He has pushed past many low expectations that others have set for him. Quinn, now sixteen, explains:

> When I was five years old, I met a lady who had a guide dog. My mom called every guide dog school, and they all said, "Call back when Quinn is seventeen, and when he's eighteen, he can have a dog." Finally Mom heard of a guide dog school in Montreal, Canada, that had given a dog to someone younger than eighteen.
>
> I had to come for a weeklong assessment. It was intense. They would test me on walking with my cane from eight in the morning to four in the afternoon. They had to know that I could cross a four-way stop intersection and a traffic light intersection on the city's busiest street. They would drop me off with a walkie-talkie and tell me to find my way back. It was tough. Everyone else could ask for directions, but I didn't speak French. It was sink or swim, and I didn't want to sink; so I dog-paddled.
>
> They told me I would be the first kid from the United States to receive one of their dogs. My dog would speak French, and I had to learn the language fast. The summer of 2003, I flew back to Montreal for five weeks. There was a three-day bonding period where they put me in a room with a lot of dogs and let me explore. They did a work session to see which dog would work with me best. I was paired with a black lab named Coda. I took Coda back to my room to sleep by my bed, and the next day, she knew I was her owner.

Quinn and Coda flew home together—the first teenage boy–dog team in the country. When they stepped off the plane, reporters were waiting for them. Quinn and his family wanted to do something positive with that media attention. They decided to create a service dog school in the United States that would accept applicants from middle school–age and up.

Why don't kids usually get dogs? Quinn explains:

> The theory is kids are not responsible enough. It costs about $25,000 to raise and train a guide dog from the time it is born till it is matched with an owner. You have to be very diligent to help your dog stay trained, and your family has to be responsible too. I feel maybe some kids can't handle a dog, but you can't judge all kids together. You have to look at them individually.
>
> I've walked into glass doors and fallen down steps. Working with Coda gives me a feeling of safety. Parking lots used to make me afraid. Standing next to a busy street, I used to hear the cars and trucks and think, "What if one of them doesn't see me?" Walking with a cane is fine from the knees down, but it won't protect you from higher objects sticking into your path. I did a lot of research on guide dogs and how they help you. Having a dog of my own was my dream.
>
> I want to tell the world that you can do anything you want to. Before Coda, I was a shy, timid kid, afraid to explore my own yard. But what I had to do to get Coda helped me grow. I came back from Montreal with confidence. I feel free. I can go to a basketball game with my friends or to McDonalds. I can just walk up to the counter and order my food, and Coda will take me to an empty seat. Now I have more friends, and Coda is a girl magnet.[15]

You can learn more about Quinn's service dog school at www.qhfoundation.org.

TTY portable phone. Courtesy of Ultratec.

year. TRS services can be accessed by dialing 711 anywhere in the United States, and the relay service is free.

TTYs can be further adapted with a Braille display such as TeleBraille from Freedom Scientific, which combines a standard TTY with a Braille display and is made portable with a battery pack.

VOICE RECOGNITION SOFTWARE

Voice recognition software lets you use your voice to control your computer. The four most popular commercial speech recognition software programs are Dragon NaturallySpeaking, IBM ViaVoice, L&H VoiceXpress, and Philips FreeSpeech. This software can be used to dictate text or give commands; users can edit and format by voice, cut and paste, open

MICH GERSON: PLUGGED IN

A full and fast-paced day begins for Mich Gerson when her Sonic Boom alarm clock with bed shaker kicks in. A second-year professional and technical communications major at Rochester Institute of Technology, Mich has been deaf since she was three and a half. She chose RIT because she feels comfortable with the Deaf community at RIT's National Technical Institute for the Deaf. The Boom is just one of the high-tech tools she uses to juggle a sixteen-credit course load, a job, executive board positions on two organizations, and an active social life.

Besides a vibrating alarm clock, I have a T-Mobile Sidekick cell phone that I use to communicate. The Sidekick allows me to text if I need to, so now I can contact my friends and parents anytime, anywhere. My room has a strobe doorbell light, so when someone rings the bell, this—quite annoying—flasher goes off. I have a similar one for fire alarms.

I also have this beautiful Dell laptop that I abuse—if I'm in my room, I am most likely on it, talking on AIM and e-mail. I use computer-mediated communication more than I use face-to-face communication—how sad is that? But with my schedule being as hectic as it is, sometimes that's the best.

I use closed-captions on TVs, or subtitles for DVDs, when I watch TV/movies. I enjoy movies to no end. I'm a huge chick flick fan, and I'm also a reality TV junkie. Name any reality TV show, and I've probably watched it. Here in Rochester, they have a movie theater that shows a movie with subtitles every week, and you can bet the movie theater is packed when a new subtitled movie comes out.

I also use C-Print in class, but not too often. [C-Print is a speech-to-text transcription system used at many schools. It was developed at the National Technical Institute for the Deaf, which is part of RIT. As the professor lectures, a trained captionist types the words into a laptop and the input is displayed simultaneously on Deaf students' monitors. If a Deaf student has a question, he or she types it into the laptop, and the captionist voices it.] I prefer a sign language interpreter because I love participating in class, and C-Print is *really* slow, which makes it hard to use. C-Print does not allow me to participate in class. I love speaking up. I love voicing my opinion, and I love contributing to class discussions, and as great as C-Print is, it just doesn't allow me to be part of the classroom. I feel like I stick out like a sore thumb when I use C-Print—even more so if I'm the only Deaf person in the classroom. But if by some stroke of luck I get both, I use C-Print to print out the notes the next day—the entire class lecture on paper! Who would not like that?[16]

programs, close windows, create e-mail, and surf the Web. The newer continuous-speech voice recognition programs can recognize speech at up to 160 words a minute.

This software doesn't *really* understand you. If you tell your dictation program about the rotten date you had last night, it doesn't care—but it will learn to recognize your specific voice and vocabulary. As you speak, it remembers the way you say each word. It can also study your phrasing and predict what word you wish to input. But voice recognition is not perfect yet, and some users still experience problems with accuracy.

WORD PREDICTION SOFTWARE

Word prediction software can really help individuals who have difficulty controlling their hands but who want to use a regular keyboard. Word prediction helps with spelling, word choice, and sentence construction. As the user types, the software applies advanced word prediction, grammatical and phonetic algorithms to complete words and predict future words to enable the user to type correctly spelled words and phrases more quickly, or for a longer time with less effort.

RESOURCES

Able Project.org is a nonprofit network where people with disabilities can research, compare, locate, and obtain mobility and assistive products. www.ableproject.org/ableproject

ABLEDATA provides objective information about assistive technology products and rehabilitation equipment available from domestic and international sources. ABLEDATA does not sell any products, but the site can help you locate companies that do. www.abledata.com

The Alexander Graham Bell Association for the Deaf and Hard of Hearing offers a list of auditory and assistive listening devices. www.agbell.org/DesktopDefault.aspx?p=Hearing_Technology

Cameron Clapp, a teenage triple amputee, has a great website. He says, "On September 15, 2001, 4 days after the tragedy of 9/11, my 15 year old life changed forever as I experienced a tragedy of my own. I was hit by a train, resulting in the loss of three limbs—one arm and both legs above the knee. Remarkably, my head and body escaped the accident with hardly a scratch. For that I am very grateful." cameronclapp.com/home.asp

SIGN LANGUAGE GLOVE

Inspiration struck Ryan Patterson, an eighteen-year-old student at Central High School in Grand Junction, Colorado, while he was downing a fast-food burger and fries.

> **I was trying to think of a science fair project to do, and I thought, "What have I seen over the past year that I can try to improve? What needs to be done?" Then I remembered a time when I was at the same restaurant and saw some people who were deaf who needed an interpreter to help them place their order. I thought I could try to develop an electronic method that would make it easier for people to communicate.**

Seven months later—and one day before the Western Colorado Science Fair—Patterson completed a prototype glove that can translate the hand positions employed by people who use American Sign Language to fingerspell words in English by converting then into large, easy-to-read letters displayed on a computer screen. Patterson's glove offers a new way in which individuals who sign can express themselves during brief conversations with people who don't understand sign language.

Patterson's invention, the Sign Language Translator, was a Grand Award winner in the 2001 Intel International Science and Engineering Fair, where it was named best in category of engineering, and the first-place winner in the individual category at the 2001 Siemens Westinghouse Science & Technology Competition. On March 11, 2001, Patterson received top honors and a $100,000 scholarship at Intel's Science Talent Search, a competition often referred to as the "junior Nobel prize."

Dr. James Battey, director of National Institute on Deafness and Other Communication Disorders (NIDCD), says:

> **New assistive technologies hold tremendous promise in helping people with communication disorders interact more easily in everyday settings. We at NIDCD are delighted that a talented and creative young person like Ryan is interested in contributing his skill to challenges of human communication. We hope to do all that we can to nurture the interests of young scientists.[17]**

Ryan Patterson and his invention, the Sign Language Translator. Courtesy of the National Institute of Deafness and Other Communication Disorders.

The National Eye Institute is part of the National Institutes of Health and is a compendium of blind and low-vision resources. www.nei.nih.gov/index.asp

NOTES

1. Statia Wilson, interview with author, July 13, 2005.
2. Michael Hineberg, interview with author, October 20, 2005.
3. National Limb Loss Information Center, "National Limb Loss Information Center Fact Sheet: Amputation Statistics by Cause: Limb Loss in the United States," www.amputee-coalition.org/fact_sheets/amp_stats_cause.html (November 28, 2006).
4. Ossur Rheo Knee website, www.ossur.com/template110.asp?PageID=1780 (October 6, 2005).
5. Motion Control website, www.utaharm.com (October 10, 2005).
6. Courtney Glodowski, telephone interview with author, August 29, 1005.
7. Tanya Holton, telephone interview with author October 14, 2005.
8. Mike Tindell, interview with author, October 19, 2005.
9. Justin Fegel, interview with author, October 10, 2005.
10. Freedom Scientific website, www.freedomscientific.com (October 31, 2005).
11. Fegel, interview with author, October 10, 2005.
12. Fegel, interview with author, October 10, 2005.
13. Yahoo Messenger with Voice website, messenger.yahoo.com/feat_voice.php;_ylt=AtRoJClrzeoCy2fMJfJ0x61wMMIF (September 2005).
14. Annie Connor, interview with author, April 13, 2005.
15. Quinn Haberl, interview with author, April 11, 2005.
16. Mich Gerson, e-mail, October 12, 2005.
17. Ryan's story comes from the National Institute on Deafness and Other Communication Disorders, "Teenage Inventor Brings Sign-Translating Glove to NIDCD," March 19, 2002, www.nidcd.nih.gov/news/releases/02/3_19_02.htm (February 3, 2006).

Getting There: Around the Block— Around the World

AROUND THE BLOCK

"Just because I can't see the stars doesn't mean I can't reach for them."

—Quinn Haberl, 16[1]

Amanda broke her neck in a diving accident the day after her fifteenth birthday. She uses her chair at all times. Shawna had cancer, and her leg had to be amputated. She uses a sports chair to play wheelchair basketball but usually she walks with an artificial limb. Alex was in an auto-bike accident as a toddler. His active life gives his many chairs a beating: "I'm sitting on an Eagle right now, and it's a bit of a pile. I want a Quickie T. It's made of titanium, and it's so light it's incredible." Jessie was born with cerebral palsy. Her chair is purple and powered. With a swivel of the joystick she can lay back and relax, or unfold into a standing position.

Two of humankind's earliest inventions were the chair and the wheel. Putting the two together has helped people get around for centuries, but wheelchair technology really took off after World War II, when returning veterans created a massive demand. The wheelchair's image has improved too. There was a time when people confined to wheelchairs didn't like to go out much in public.

Franklin D. Roosevelt, president of the United States for much of World War II, contracted polio when he was thirty-nine. He was never able to walk again, but he was very careful to stand for public appearances, even though it was grueling and painful. If he were president today, along with Air Force One, he would have Wheelchair One, and it would be a high-powered machine. People with disabilities are demanding mobility and the freedom that comes with it. To achieve their demands, technology is being pushed to new limits.

If you need a power chair, you are living at the right time. Six-wheel power chairs are taking maneuverability to new levels. Two big drive wheels sit directly below the chair, while two casters each in front and back stabilize it. Innovation in Motion's X-5 Frontier chair can pivot on a dime.

"It's an indoor wheelchair with aggressive outdoor capability," says Rick Michael, vice president of Innovation in Motion, which imports the chairs from Australia. "It's the

A rare photo of President Franklin D. Roosevelt in his wheelchair. Courtesy of the Franklin D. Roosevelt Presidential Library.

conventional wheelchair on steroids. It can handle sand, snow, and mud. It will climb up over a four-inch curb."

Michael compares wheelchair progress to development in cars from the Model T to the Miata. "Now there are wheelchairs to fit everyone's needs," he says. "It's a matter of what you want to accomplish. There is something out there for you. People are asking more and more of their wheelchairs. You want to go where everyone else is going. You want progress."

An able-bodied person can stride, skip, or slouch down the street, sending powerful messages about who she is to the people who see her. In the past, people in wheelchairs have had to deal with the fact that the first thing others are likely to notice about them is their wheels, and until recently the chairs gave off stodgy "hospital" vibes. Finally, wheelchair design is beginning to catch up.

"People don't want to look like they are in a wheelchair," Michael continues. "That's the beauty of these modern chairs. You can get something that is sporty and reflects your personality. It's like a pair of fun shoes or jeans. You want something that has not only functionality, but personality."[2]

Technology is moving beyond standard wheelchairs with inventions like the INDEPENDENCE iBOT 4000 Mobility System. The iBOT 4000 uses multiple built-in computers that work with gyroscopes. Gyroscopes are motion sensors that help maintain balance. When the gyroscopes sense movement, they send a signal to the computers, which process the information and tell the motors how to move the wheels to maintain stability. In balance mode, this device can put you eye to eye with your friends as the front wheels rotate up and over the back wheels. You remain seated, but at a higher level. It can climb up and down stairs, hop curbs as high as five inches, and travel over uneven terrain, such as sand, gravel, grass, and thick carpet.[3]

Megan Yekel is a tenth-grader who has been using mobility devices since 1999 when she was first diagnosed with muscular dystrophy. "My mom was the first one to recognize that the iBOT might be the best chair for me when she saw it on Dateline NBC," Megan says. "When I first got the iBOT, I immediately went to see my grandparents and uncles, who were able to hug me while they were standing up. I love the hugging thing. At school my classmates were all amazed and asked a million questions.

"My school is very old and not accessible. There are no elevators at all. The chemistry room is located on a higher floor, so with the stairs involved, I could not go to the lab. Now, for the first time, I can attend it. I can give presentations in class while in the balance mode. It puts me at eye level with my teachers. The other cool thing is that I am able to reach my locker, which is such a relief.

Megan Yekel can reach any shelf from her iBOT. Courtesy of Independence Technology LLC.

"I love music, and I often go to the concerts of cool local bands, where now I can stand in the back row while in balance mode and still have a great view. I don't have to be in the front row anymore, blocking the view of others. With the iBOT, I can tool around my high school, visit family, friends, and interact with other students at eye level. I feel like I finally fit in—I blend with the crowd."[4]

DRIVING IMPULSE

When you turn sixteen with a physical disability, you hit a major fork in the road. Driving is a huge deal. That little plastic card with your picture on it is the key to the kingdom. Kids who have one can get into their cars and can go where they want. If you can't drive, it's easy to feel like you have been sidetracked to a dead-end dirt road.

"It all comes back to transportation," says Katy Sandberg, a college junior with cerebral palsy. "I'll never be able to drive because of my spasms. It's a pain. A lot of my friends go to college only three hours away, and if I wasn't in a chair, I could get to see them easily. But it is hard to do anything outside of my school and my town."[5]

Unless you are free to travel where and when you want, you face challenges getting to school, looking for work, or hanging out with your friends. What you find in the way of public transportation is going to vary from city to city and state to state. The ability to drive makes so many things possible.

On the other hand, you've seen the headlines—driving is dangerous. It can lead to serious injury and even death. Driving is a complex task. The privilege of getting behind the wheel will take some planning and will probably involve evaluation, testing, adaptations, and a lot of experimentation to see what works for you.

The Association for Driver Rehabilitation Specialists is a good place to get help if you are wondering if and how you can drive. (You can find its website at the end of this chapter.) A driver rehabilitation evaluation can estimate your strengths and weaknesses behind the wheel.

Let's look at some of the driving options out there.

Motion Impairment and Driving

To drive a sedan, you've got to be able to lock and unlock the car, open and close the door, transfer yourself to and from a wheelchair, and get your chair in and out of the car. If you can't manage these things, a van may be a driving option because specialized modifications can help you transfer to the driver's seat or even allow you to drive from your wheelchair.

Driving controls can be adapted if you don't have the strength or range of motion usually needed to drive a car. Reduced-effort steering systems are available, and servo-boosted brake and accelerator controls take less strength to use. Joystick driving systems require only one hand to operate the brake, accelerator, and steering. A spinner knob attached to the steering wheel lets you steer with one hand, or a left gas pedal can be used if you can't use your right foot.

"I'd be lost without a vehicle," says Angela, who is paralyzed from the chest down. She drives a Dodge Caravan with Braun Entervan conversion. "Being in a power chair, I

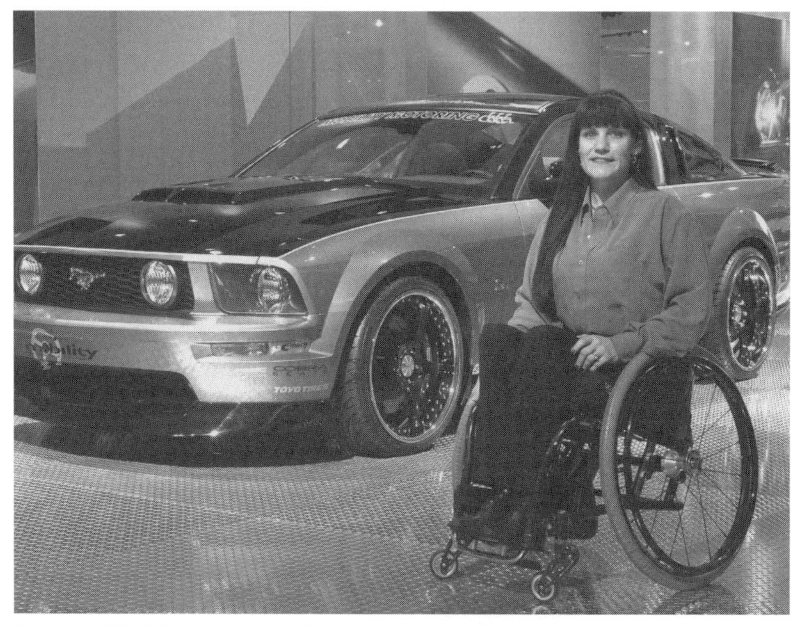

Carol Hollfelder races her Ford Mustang with specially engineered hand controls. Courtesy of Ford Mobility Motoring.

can't just transfer into the car and load in my chair. It's all operated by remote control. When I come up to the car, I push a button, and the door opens on the passenger side, and a ramp comes down. I drive up the ramp. The driver's seat turns 90 degrees, and I transfer and spin it to face forward. I use hand controls and because my fingers are paralyzed, I have a tri-pin steering device—three pins arranged in a triangle. My fingers go around the top pin, and the bottom pins hold my wrist in place."[6]

Alex McKenzie, a college junior majoring in psychology, lost the use of his legs in an accident when he was four. He gets around in a regular Subaru Impreza sport wagon that has been modified for him.

"I've got hand controls," he explains. "I do the gas and brake with my left hand. You push forward for brakes, and the gas is kind of like a motorcycle. You twist your wrist to accelerate, and I've got a steering knob so I can steer with one hand. They work pretty smoothly."

Alex went through driver's ed at his school and took the standardized driver's test to get his license. The only driving conditions he doesn't like are the slushy, snowy roads he sees in Wisconsin winters.

"I get in the driver's seat and take the wheels off my chair and put them in the back," he says. "Then I lift my chair

Mario Solis uses his Ford Expedition to carry his sports equipment. Courtesy of Ford Mobility Motoring.

AVIS ACCESS

In 2003 the rental-car company Avis announced the nation's first comprehensive accessibility program for travelers with disabilities. Avis Access is targeted to reach the 54 million Americans with mobility, hearing, or visual impairments.

Specifically, Avis Access provides a dedicated twenty-four-hour toll-free number for customers with special travel needs, along with TTY/TDD access for those with a hearing impairment. Other specific service offerings for drivers and passengers with disabilities include the following complimentary service options:

- Transfer Board: Eases the driver or passenger from his wheelchair into the car seat.
- Swivel Seat: Allows the driver or passenger to turn her body in the car seat with limited effort. The seat can easily be removed from underneath the person.
- Spinner Knob: Enables a full turning radius of the steering wheel while using only one hand.
- Panoramic Mirror: Provides a much larger field of view for any driver, and is a legal requirement for hearing-impaired drivers.
- Hand Controls: Lets drivers with limited leg function accelerate or brake using a hand-controlled device. Controls do not interfere with drivers who are not physically challenged.
- Accessible Bus Service: Offers an electrically operated ramp or lift, two ADA-compliant wheelchair positions, special aisles, and low luggage racks.
- Additional Driver Fee Waiver: Customers with visual impairment can rent an Avis car without incurring any additional driver fees for their designated driver. (All drivers must meet Avis' standard licensed driver requirements.)

"The Avis Access Program is a beacon in the tourism, hospitality, and rental car sectors for all companies to learn from and follow," says Eric Lipp, executive director of the nonprofit Open Doors Organization.[7]

over me and put it in the passenger seat. If I'm with someone, I have them throw my chair in the back with the wheels on. Either way, it gets pretty dirty with all that slush in the back seat.

"A lot of car companies will help you out with adapted controls. My adaptations cost $700. When we bought the car and told them we were going to get it adapted, they refunded us $500."[8]

Most automakers have similar adaptive programs, such as the mobility programs offered by Ford and GM. A driver rehabilitation specialist can help you find the right vehicle with the right equipment once it is determined that you have the ability to drive.

Visually Impaired Driving

Each state has its own vision requirements for driving. A common requirement is 20/40 acuity with best spectacle

WHAT DOES 20/20 VISION MEAN?

To have 20/20 vision means that if you stand twenty feet away from an eye chart, you can see what a "normal" person can see. Of course "normal" is very hard to define. In this case, because most people have 20/20 vision, it's a case of majority rules. If you have 20/40 vision, that means you can see at twenty feet what the hypothetical "normal" person can see from forty feet. If you have 20/100 vision, when you stand twenty feet from the eye chart, you can see what the "normal" person can see from one hundred feet away. Anyone with vision worse than 20/200 that cannot be improved with corrective lenses is considered legally blind.

correction or contact lenses to drive day and night, and 20/70 to drive only during daylight. (Daylight is defined as from sunrise to sunset.) Individuals whose vision corrects to less than 20/40 acuity may be able to use a spectacle-mounted telescopic device to meet the vision requirement. Drivers also have to meet the required visual field. Peripheral vision can be more important than central acuity in driving safely. An individual who has tunnel vision won't see things coming from the sides and won't be able to drive safely.

Driving with Hearing Impairment

"I find I can drive just fine," says Dan, who has been almost totally deaf since age three. He says he misses the extra cues that sound can give you much more when bicycling or walking in the dark.

It is perfectly legal to drive with a hearing impairment, but you need to take extra care to be constantly aware of your surroundings. Check your mirrors often for police cars, fire trucks, and ambulances with emergency lights flashing.

If you are stopped by the police, keep your hands on the steering wheel. You may be reaching for a pencil and paper, but to a nervous police officer, it may seem like you are reaching for a weapon. Let the officer recognize that you are deaf or hard of hearing. It can be stressful and difficult to communicate with a police officer, especially if the officer involved has not had enough training in disability awareness. Be prepared to meet the officer more than halfway.

Safety First

Individuals taking the test for a driver's license have to show that they have skills that include vehicle speed control, shifting and braking, depth and spatial perception, steering, use of mirrors, backing up and parking, as well as knowledge of the rules of the road and courtesy. Driving is a privilege, not a right. Getting behind the wheel means taking your life and the lives of others into your hands. You must always be aware that your safety margin is reduced because your disability may mean it takes you longer to spot and respond to hazards. Choose the safest route before hand. Know where you are going before you put the key in the ignition. As a driver with a physical disability, you must have an especially strong sense of responsibility to judge how your disability combines with weather, traffic, and other conditions at all times, and you must be prepared to say, "I can't drive right now."

The cost of modifying your car can vary greatly. According to the National Highway Traffic Safety Administration, a new vehicle modified with adaptive equipment can cost as much as $80,000, so it pays to explore every opportunity for financial assistance. There are programs that can help pay for part or all of the costs of modification, depending on the cause and nature of your disability. For information, contact your state's Department of Vocational Rehabilitation. Many nonprofit associations have grant programs to help pay for adaptive devices, and many automakers have rebate or reimbursement plans for modified automobiles.

Off-road wheelchairs. Courtesy of Innovation in Motion.

TRAVEL BY PLANE

Sometimes the best way to get from point A to point B is to climb forty thousand feet in the air and barrel along at 550 miles per hour. About 800 million passengers take to the skies worldwide every year. A lot of those passengers complain that planes feel more and more like cattle cars with wings, but if you have a physical disability you probably have more to complain about than most.

"Airplane travel is very difficult," says Rebecca Wylie, a quadriplegic student at the University of Missouri whose home is in Illinois. "I've flown four times, and all four trips I had problems. They put the wheelchair in cargo, and they don't seem to understand that my wheelchair is my legs. They don't get it. They don't care. Plus they are not trained how to pick up a wheelchair and put it in cargo. They pile boxes and luggage around it. Sometimes it is too tall and doesn't fit in the door, so we have to take its back off. It's very sensitive. They bend the seat, and then the chair doesn't work electronically. Once, we had to call a wheelchair guy to come to our hotel room to get it fixed.

"We tried everything. We talked to the guy who was going to put it on the airplane. My mom has called all the airlines, and she wants to speak to someone about training their employees. I would be more than willing to run a symposium or better yet, get wheelchairs placed in the plane.

"It's kind of a weird thing. The airlines are fine with paying for damages, but it ruins vacations. Luckily, mine has never been completely damaged, but I've heard of other people whose wheelchairs have been totaled during travel, and they have to wait as much as a year to get a new one. That's why I picked University of Missouri. I can use Amtrak, which allows wheelchairs."[9]

If you have a visual impairment, an airport offers a different set of hurdles to scale on the way to the plane.

Goalball coach Jackie Pieper travels with her team to games around the country. She acts as a sighted guide for the team. "Often our day-to-day world is not built for people with visual impairment," Jackie says. "They need large, high-contrast signs, not designer color schemes. What is really pleasing to the sighted population can be extremely difficult to see if you have a visual impairment. When you see blue signs for the bathroom on a gray wall, most of my team could not find that.

"Then there is the small print on airline tickets and boarding passes. And of course there is getting to the plane when they may not be able to read the gate numbers, and then finding directions to their seat."[10]

Eric Lipp, founder and director of the Open Doors Organization, works to bridge the gap between business, including the travel industry, and the disability community. He commissioned a study on travel, hospitality, and entertainment spending by people with disabilities.

According to the latest available census figures, in 1995 there were about 48.5 million people over the age of fifteen with a disability in the United States, and they spent a whopping $81.7 billion on travel in that year alone. According to Lipp, that kind of spending will someday generate more attention to the needs of travelers with disabilities.

"In the meantime, expect the unexpected," Lipp advises travelers with disabilities. "It's hard to grasp what it will be like because no two airports are the same, and no two airlines will treat you the same way.

"Some of the main obstacles to air travel are just navigating the airport. Finding elevators if you use a chair, finding raised lettering if you are blind, hearing the announcements if you are deaf. A lot of teens may be shy to ask questions. As we get older we learn to ask right away.

"Plan early. People with disabilities have to go through extra stages in planning, but the new security has actually made it better. Having skilled employees in security has created a high level of personal service."[11]

The Transportation Security Administration (TSA), a division within the Department of Homeland Security, has posted updated information for air travelers, including those with disabilities, on security screening procedures. This information explains the rights of passengers with disabilities. These tips are posted on the TSA's website at www.tsa.gov.

TRAVEL BY TRAIN

Most Amtrak stations in major cities and some smaller stations across the country are accessible to passengers with disabilities. As the company builds new stations and renovates old ones, Amtrak's goal is to make every station accessible by 2010.

Amtrak can offer wheelchair space, transfer seats (for passengers who travel in a seat and stow their wheelchairs), and accessible sleeper accommodations. All trains with meal service allow customers with disabilities to order from the menu and have their meals served at their seats or in their rooms. Amtrak also offers a rail fare discount to passengers with disabilities. As always, traveling with a disability means a lot of planning ahead. Travelers need to reserve services as far in advance as possible because accessible space is limited. To get the most up-to-date information about accessibility of the stations on your trip, call 1 800-USA-RAIL (1 800-872-7245).

TRAVEL BY BUS

What is available to you in public transportation depends on where you live. Keep in mind that the Americans with Disabilities Act (ADA) of 1990 requires public transit agencies

I believe that all people with disabilities are members of a global family. Working together across borders is our most powerful way of effecting changes.
—Susan Sygall, CEO, Mobility International USA (MIUSA)

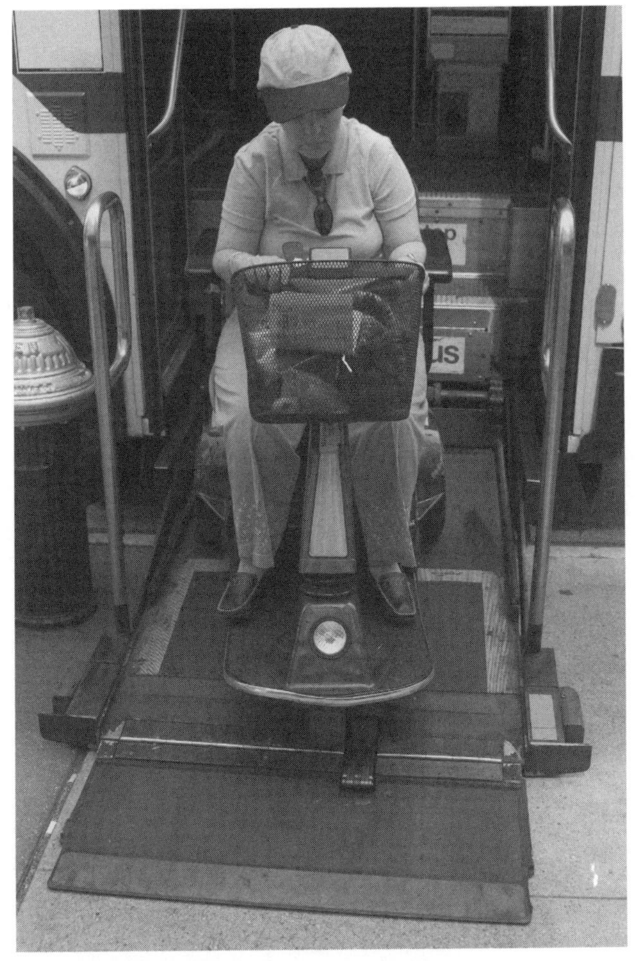

Get on the bus. Courtesy of iStockphoto.

to provide Paratransit Service to those who cannot access the public transit system due to disability. Paratransit is a service where individuals who are unable to use the regular transit system independently (because of a physical or mental impairment) are picked up and dropped off at their destinations.

What ADA says specifically is: Public transportation authorities may not discriminate against you. They must comply with requirements for accessibility in newly purchased vehicles, make good-faith efforts to purchase or lease accessible used buses, remanufacture buses in an accessible manner, and, unless it would result in an undue burden, provide Paratransit where they operate fixed-route bus or rail systems. Questions and complaints about public transportation may be directed to the U.S. Department of Transportation Federal Transit Administration's Office of Civil Rights by calling (888) 446-4511 (voice/relay) Another good resource is Project ACTION, a national program that supports innovation and cooperation in solving transit accessibility problems. It maintains a library of information and materials on accessible transportation for people with disabilities. Check out the program's website at www.projectaction.org.

CHALLENGE YOURSELF AND CHANGE THE WORLD

"Challenge Yourself and Change the World" is the rallying cry of Mobility International USA, an organization that can help you find a travel program that works for you. MIUSA's National Clearinghouse on Disability and Exchange is sponsored by the Bureau of Education and Cultural Affairs of the U.S. Department of State.

MIUSA offers international exchange programs that last from two to four weeks and are held throughout the year in the United States and abroad. The program has involved people with and without disabilities from more than eighty countries. Activities include living with homestay families, leadership seminars, disability rights workshops, cross-cultural learning, and team-building activities such as river rafting and challenge courses. Participants develop strategies for making changes, both within themselves and in their communities.

MIUSA can help you connect with a range of international volunteer, study, work, and research programs. And its peer network of more than three hundred people who have traveled already can tell you what to expect, what to bring, and what you need to know.

LOOK OUT, WORLD—HERE I COME!

Travel will give you a leg up in life. "I am a college-educated person with many experiences. I worked my way through college, and I've had an internship, but that doesn't make me stand out," says Melissa Mitchell, outreach and training coordinator for the National Clearinghouse on Disability and Exchange. "That's not enough to rise to the top of the pile. What blows prospective employers out of the water is my international experience."

According to Mitchell, international experience is a great way to build the skills you will need as an independent adult:

- **Flexibility and adaptability are skills you will need in any job. How do you get your needs met in a different culture? What do you do if your chair breaks? Problem solving on the fly will come in handy over and over.**
- **Budget skills. As a traveler, you have to manage your money for unexpected problems and opportunities. This is crucial for life, and a great job skill.**
- **Orientation skills. You must learn quickly how to find your way through unfamiliar terrain. The ability to ask for and understand directions is a worthwhile skill.**
- **Time management. In the school of life, time management is taught pass/fail. If you show up late—the train is gone.**

On the trail. Photo by author.

A big advantage to traveling with a disability, says Mitchell, is that "[y]ou learn what your actual limitations are—not what other people have told you they are, and not what you assume they are. You will also learn what your capabilities are. You will realize that there were some things that your friends and family were just doing for you as an unspoken thing. You get comfortable and take it for granted until it's not there.

"When we send people traveling, we ask them what kind of accommodations they need. We ask them, 'What would you need if we took you tent camping?' That way they can frame in their mind what they really need.

"Travel will make you more confident and build your self-advocacy skills. Parents and teachers are always trying to teach self-determination, but it's really hard to practice those skills in your home environment. People know what you need and how to work with you. Your needs are usually being met. Besides, you are working with people you may have known for years, and you don't want to hurt their feelings. It's easier to practice being assertive in a travel setting because you are interacting with people you won't see again.

"In a different culture, people don't know you, and what you can and can't do. If you don't speak up, they assume there isn't a problem. If you want to participate in society, self-advocacy skills are absolutely necessary. On the road, your choices have consequences. If you don't speak up for yourself, who is going to?"

Travel is a really interesting experiment in cause and effect. This is how we learn. These are important experiences for everyone to have, but even more so for people with disabilities. You have issues—medical issues, equipment issues, issues of care. You have to learn how to take care of these things wherever you are: how to order a chair, how to pick a personal assistant, how to navigate the system. This is a part of your life, and you have to know how to make it work. It gives you a sense of empowerment.

"It's not all about what you will get from international travel," says Mitchell. "It's even more about what you will give.

ONE WOMAN'S JOURNEY

Melissa Mitchell has cerebral palsy and uses a wheelchair. She says:

> I've been traveling by myself since I was eight years old. I went by myself to Arizona to see my grandma when I was eight. I'm sure my mother was terrified, but it was a thing in our family that all the kids got to visit grandma alone, and she wasn't taking no for an answer just because I was in a chair. That's how I got the travel bug.
>
> The first time I traveled to Europe was for a French immersion program in college. I traveled with a friend of mine who was a little younger than me. It was funny. At the airport, her parents turned to me and said, "You take care of her." Usually people are worried about someone taking care of me.
>
> After a seventeen-hour flight from Seattle to Paris our adventure began. I got in my chair, and it felt awfully strange. We grabbed a taxi, got to the train station, and they couldn't put my chair back together. I sat down on the sidewalk with the chair thinking, "I'll show them." Then I saw the problem. The axle is supposed to be straight. It was far from straight. I had no idea what to do. Nothing like this had ever happened to my chair.

Melissa Mitchell traveling in Europe. Photo courtesy of Melissa Mitchell.

(*continued*)

ONE WOMAN'S JOURNEY (*continued*)

When we got to our host family, I tried to explain what happened to my chair. They don't teach you this vocabulary in French class. I called the airport, but they said that because I left the airport without complaining, they were not responsible. My host family found me a hospital-type wheelchair, so I spent the month in a borrowed chair. We made it work.

We made a field trip to a basin carved out by a waterfall. Tourists can go to the top on a donkey to see the view. We watched them put a toddler on a donkey, but then they said, "We're not putting you on a donkey." I wasn't about to miss out on this when I'd just seen a two-year old could do it. We started making a fuss as loudly as we could in every language we knew. We finally got them to back down. It was awfully beautiful up there, and I wouldn't trade that ride for the world.

I almost didn't go on that trip because they were having a hard time finding me a host family. That can be pretty common. When I went back to France as a foreign-language teacher assistant, they first placed me in a high school, but—whoops!—the high school was not wheelchair accessible. Instead they placed me in a university in Normandy and let me have university housing. The weather there is wet, rainy, and cold. Being that close to my workplace turned out to be a good thing.

So far, I've made it to France, Spain, and Canada, and I've visited about half of the states. I'm planning to go to Tanzania next. I've always wanted to.

I can't imagine a better way than travel for anyone to come up with a true self-concept. Once you take yourself out of your native culture, where you know the rules of the game, and you plop yourself down in Bizzaroland, where the next step you make may be the biggest mistake of your life—that's when you find out what is true about you.[12]

"When I traveled abroad the second time, I worked with two elementary classes because both of them had children in wheelchairs. It was important for them to see me traveling independently. It's important for everyone to see it.

"That is how we become truly accepted. If we really want a world where everyone is equal, and where disability is seen for what it is—a natural part of the human condition—we have to get out there. We have to be seen. We have to be heard. We have to participate.

"Sure, everybody in your neighborhood knows what you can do, but do you want to live in a safety bubble? Do you want to see the rest of the world? Can you do it? You won't know until you go and experience it."[13]

RESOURCES

Alexander Graham Bell Association for the Deaf and Hard of Hearing has some good info on driving. www.hearourvoices.org/DesktopDefault.aspx?p=Driving_Deaf

The Association for Driver Rehabilitation Specialists (ADED) is a good source of information about transportation equipment modifications for persons with disabilities. www.driver-ed.org

Infinitec.org offers a smattering of popular places to visit in the United States and stops beyond. You'll be surprised at the variety of places already scoped out for disabled travelers. www.infinitec.org/play/travel/coolplaces.htm

Mobility International USA offers many opportunities for international travel for people with disabilities. www.miusa.org

The National Highway Traffic Safety Administration. This site has a compendium of information on adapting cars for people with disabilities. www.nhtsa.dot.gov/cars/rules/adaptive/brochure/brochure.html#Anchor-49575

The National Mobility Equipment Dealers Association (NMEDA). This site can help you locate a mobility dealer in your area and help you make the best choices for your transportation needs. www.nmeda.org

NOTES

1. Quinn Haberl, interview with author, April 11, 2005.
2. Rick Michael, interview with author, October 6, 2005.
3. Independence iBOT 4000 Mobility System website, www.independencenow.com/ibot (October 19, 2006).
4. iBOT Mobility System, "iBOT® Experiences—Megan," www.ibotnow.com/ibot/megan.html (October 19, 2006).

5. Katy Sandberg, telephone interview with author, September 22, 2005.

6. Angela Kuemmel, interview with author, September 28, 2005.

7. Society for Accessible Travel & Hospitality, "Avis Rent A Car Launches 'Avis Access' for Travelers with Disabilities," October 2003, www.sath.org/index.html?pageID=3665&-session=thisSession:5878ADEDDF14253C98AA857A7B771CA0 (October 19, 2006).

8. Alex McKenzie, interview with author, August 26, 2005.

9. Rebecca Wylie, interview with author, October 17, 2003.

10. Jackie Pieper, interview with author, October 14, 2003.

11. Eric Lipp, interview with author October 17, 2003.

12. Melissa Mitchell, interview with author, November 26, 2005.

13. Mitchell, interview with author, November 26, 2005.

Getting into the Game: Sports and Recreation

Changing attitudes and better equipment are getting people with disabilities off the sidelines. Picture a world in which people with disabilities have the same opportunities to discover their athletic potential and pursue their dreams as able-bodied people. It is happening!

"Life is not a spectator sport. It's participatory and it's for everybody."
—Mike Froggly, head wheelchair basketball coach, University of Illinois, Urbana-Champaign[1]

Adapted sports give kids with disabilities the chance to socialize and be physically fit. They can stretch their abilities and expand their self-sufficiency. When teens with disabilities go out for sports, they are breaking the stereotypes that have painted them as weak and fragile. From judo to golf to horseback riding to basketball, teens with disabilities are getting into the game.

A GREAT EQUALIZER

High school wheelchair basketball coach Michael Van Cleve says, "Sports is a great equalizer. I've had wheelchair athletes tell me that when they are playing basketball in the school gym, ambulatory kids come up and play with them. They are changing the perceptions of how people see and react to them, and they are making ties between themselves and other students."[2]

One reason we participate in sports is the overwhelming urge to be part of something—the desire to belong. Teams pull everyone toward a common goal. Sports for teens with disabilities bring them together in a form of problem solving. It's a chance to say, "Yes, things are hard for me, too. This is how I do it."

The benefits are more than social. The surgeon general has made fighting obesity the number-one concern for youngsters. Physical activity is part of a healthy lifestyle, but being active is often more difficult for kids with disabilities.

For example, to form a wheelchair basketball team, you need more than just five people and a ball. You need sports wheelchairs. Wheelchair sports started after World War II when wheelchair-bound veterans sought an outlet for their energy. The veterans played in regulation hospital wheelchairs, but over the last ten years there has been a big push to design specialized wheelchairs for each sport. Chairs with cambered wheels (wheels that are set at an angle—top narrow, bottom wide) are easier to turn and less likely to flip. They are made of lightweight, shock-absorbent materials—and they can cost from $1,500 to $3,000.

Sixteen-year-old Carl Hamming has been in and out of his wheelchair. In sixth grade he developed a rare condition called Guillain-Barre Syndrome, which involves gradual paralysis and gradual recovery. Though he is walking again, Hamming still comes to wheelchair basketball practice. Now he comes as a teen volunteer to make sure there are enough players for a game. Wheelchair athletes often have to travel long distances, and it is difficult to gather enough players for two teams.

Not everyone recovers from Guillain-Barre Syndrome, but Hamming never doubted that he would. He says, "At first, nobody came out and told me. It was a slow process of realization. After a few months in a hospital bed, it hit me that I couldn't walk. I always believed it would be temporary, and I would be back walking soon. It took longer than I expected—two and a half years.

"Wheelchair sports helped me to play and to compete, and I loved that. I knocked people. I got flipped. It was a lot of fun. I did basketball, track and field. I tried downhill skiing. You use one ski with a seat in the middle, and you have poles that are like mini-skis about a foot long to help you balance.

"I tried tennis. You play on the same court as regular tennis. You get two bounces, but the good players don't even

Wheelchair tennis. Courtesy of iStockphoto.

use them both. The toughest part is holding a racket and wheeling your chair.

"The first chair I had was pretty junky. Then I got a sports chair, and the difference was amazing. You can spin around and flip back, but not go over. In basketball, you lean back on a special fifth wheel, and it's impossible to block you!

"When I come to practice, I feel like I connect. But I got out, and I know my friends will be in wheelchairs for the rest of their lives. It makes me feel a little guilty. At first I didn't want to come back, but now I feel prepared. It wasn't my fault I got sick, and it wasn't my fault I got better."

Hamming says he'd love to design wheelchairs someday, and he plans to be a volunteer coach. "Being in a wheelchair changed my perspective," he says. "It took the difference away."[3]

LET'S GO OUTSIDE THE LIMITS

Kids with disabilities really need to be active, says University of Illinois wheelchair basketball coach Mike Froggly: "Instead of coming up with reasons not to be active, there is a very good reason to do it—it's good for them." Froggly says that the Illinois High School Association is starting to develop wheelchair basketball as a varsity sport in the state's high schools—the first state to do so. Currently there are sixteen hundred students in Illinois ready to play. "We need other organizations around the nation to provide this kind of opportunity," Froggly says. "Let's go outside the limits. Let's open the door to imagination. There is a whole population of kids with disabilities who are beginning to ask not 'What can I watch?' but 'What can I do?'"[4]

WHO CAN PLAY WHEELCHAIR BASKETBALL?

It isn't only students who use a wheelchair on a daily basis who are eligible to play wheelchair basketball. Others who might be eligible include students with orthopedic impairments, permanent knee injuries, and leg length discrepancies, and also those students with lower extremity weakness, spinal cord injuries, spina bifida, cerebral palsy, multiple sclerosis, traumatic brain injury, or amputation. Any student who is unable to participate in able-bodied basketball may be eligible to play wheelchair basketball.

The National Junior Wheelchair Championships began in 1984. Since then, opportunities have burst out in many directions, with international competitions and junior programs in just about every sport, including track and field, archery, swimming, table tennis, and weightlifting.

Matt Scott, age twenty, is a sophomore at the University of Wisconsin, Whitewater, and arguably one of the best wheelchair basketball players in the world.

"I've always liked sports," says Matt, who was born in Detroit. He has spina bifida.

"I think Matt Scott is quite honestly one of the best athletes I've ever met in my life, and that holds true whether you are aware of the fact that he is in a wheelchair or not," says his coach, Tracy Chynoweth. The UW Whitewater wheelchair basketball team has held the number-one spot

Wheelchair basketball champion Matt Scott. Photo by author.

among U.S. college wheelchair basketball teams for three years, says Chynoweth. "There are not a lot of teams in the country, so we are all over the map."

Because Matt also plays on the USA National Wheelchair Basketball Team, he is all over the globe. He represented the United States in Athens at the 2004 Paralympics.

"I have been in Australia, England, Japan, Brazil, and Canada, but they don't count—they're just next door," says Matt. "When we are on the road, it is strictly business, but we do get to see some things. In Australia, we met with members of an aboriginal tribe.

"The main thing I notice in other countries is that they take wheelchair basketball much more seriously than we do in this country. In Athens, other countries were covering the games on television as sports news. The only coverage from the U.S. was as human interest—not sports. In Athens, there were at least five thousand people at every game. Here we are lucky to get ten or fifteen, and they are mostly family members."[5]

Chynoweth calls wheelchair basketball as interesting and intense a game as he has ever seen. "A hockey player puts on skates," he says. "My players put on wheelchairs. The wheelchair is just part of the equipment. A lot of the chairs are made of titanium. The wheels are made of carbon fiber. The wheels are tilted in, and that allows for very tight, spinning, athletic movement. They are very light and strong. They are expensive to maintain. Every person has his/her own custom-fit chair that is as important as a helmet to a football player. It's got to fit, and it's got to fit right."

Matt uses a Quickie All Court, a sport wheelchair designed by wheelchair athletes that adjusts to match each user's unique center of gravity. "The whole team uses them," says Chynoweth. "They actually sponsor our program and take very,

SPORTS SCHOLARSHIPS

There are different levels of support that come from colleges, all the way up to full-ride scholarships. The University of Texas, Arlington offers a full ride. The University of Illinois offers out-of-state waivers, but the University of Wisconsin, Whitewater can offer only small financial help, according to Froggly. He recommends wheelchair athletes contact the colleges they are interested in to learn what scholarship opportunities they may offer. "You have to keep in mind that the schools give out their scholarship money based foremost on athletic ability," Froggly adds. "They are only going to provide support if you are a skilled athlete who can contribute something to their program, in the same way you have to be a good athlete in any other program."[6]

Wheelchair racing. Courtesy of iStockphoto.

very good care of us. Mat is a sponsored athlete. He gets treated by Quickie much like Michael Jordan got treated by Nike."[7]

Seventeen-year-old Shawna Culp has been playing wheelchair basketball since fourth grade. As she remembers, "That was the summer I discovered sports. I was playing soccer, but I just couldn't run. Finally my gym teacher yelled at me and told me to get X-rayed. I had osteosarcoma, a form of bone cancer. It was decalcifying or something like that. I didn't really understand it. I was so young. I had a metal knee and a metal femur and a little bit of tibia, but it got infected when they tried to lengthen it because I was still growing, so I had an amputation.

"You don't have to be in a wheelchair all the time to play wheelchair basketball. I use a prosthetic leg. One of our players just has a knee condition. He walks most of the time. One year we had a kid with brittle bone disease.

"I love the whole thing about basketball. I love working as a team and everyone working really hard to make it all come together. The adrenaline rush—it's a great feeling.

"My team practices Fridays and Saturdays. We are a bunch of kids who want to be out having a social life, but Friday and Saturday is the only time we can get the gym. I guess you could say basketball is a part of my social life. We live so

Shawna Culp at the Illinois Wheelchair Basketball Tournament. Photo by author.

spread out that we never get together outside of basketball, but we have fun at the tournaments. We are all pretty hardcore about our sports.

"The chairs are spacey, man! They are getting lighter and quicker with new wheels. I'm on my third chair. Sometimes, if you get a really intense game going, you can actually smell the burning rubber from our wheels.

"I have the worst hands. I've got twenty-three blisters right now. I've had up to thirty-one blisters. I like to think I'm kind of tough. You are supposed to tape them up if you get blisters in a game, but I like to just push through.

"Positive attitude is a huge thing. If you have a negative attitude—you are not going to make it. The cancer doesn't kill you. You kill yourself. Even in basketball, I really feel positive energy transfer from person to person. It makes everything better."[8]

DEAF SPORT

"The Deaf community has a pretty phenomenal athletic organization," said Becki Streit, administrator of the Low Incidence Cooperative Agreement (hearing impaired program) of Northern Suburban Special Education District in the Chicago area. "Most local Deaf clubs field several athletic teams. For many kids it is their entry way into the adult Deaf community."[9]

The major international competitions for athletes who are deaf are the summer and winter Deaflympics held every four years. The Deaf community chooses to host its own sports events because in Deaf culture, hearing loss is viewed as a cultural identity rather than a physical disability in need of a cure. The term *Deaf* with a capital letter *D* is used to describe persons who identify with the Deaf culture and who

Playing four square. Courtesy of National Technical Institute for the Deaf at Rochester Institute of Technology.

use sign language as their primary mode of communication. The term *deaf* with a lowercase letter *d* is used to describe hearing loss.

At Deaf sports events, people who are deaf can communicate using sign language and see other Deaf people role modeling as athletes, coaches, officials, and volunteers.

Dan Burton became interested in sports when he decided to go to Deaf school. "I was tired being the only one who was deaf," says Dan. "Deaf school was a great experience socially, especially sports. I was competing with my peers. It was a level playing field.

"Now that I'm out of school, I've organized a Deaf disc golf club. It's a way to keep us together while we share a sport. We are hoping to get more Deaf youth—get them started in a sport early. When you are good at something, you enjoy it more.

"The thing that enthralls me about disc golfing is the solo-competition aspect. I get to challenge my physical and mental ability, and I just love watching those discs fly. It is always a rush when I hit that line just the way I visualized it."[10]

ADAPTATIONS OPEN MANY SPORTS TO THE BLIND

Kids with visual impairments also face obstacles getting involved in sports. Studies show that about half the time they aren't fully included in their school gym classes, and the less vision they have, the more they are excluded.

"The problem," says Dr. Paul Ponchillia, chairperson of the Department of Blindness and Low Vision Studies of Western Michigan University, "is that the average physical education teacher doesn't know about adaptation, and the average special education teacher doesn't know about sports. It's been a missing piece of education."[11]

In the 1980s Ponchillia developed a sports camp in Michigan for kids with visual impairment. Using a federal grant, he has started camps in twelve other states. The camps teach young athletes the rules of goalball, the only sport designed for blind people. Adaptations have also been

PARALYMPICS

The term *Paralympics* is based on the word parallel. The Paralympics are held two weeks after each regular Olympics in the same host city and using the same venues for each sport. The Paralympics is a multisport, multidisability competition of elite, world-class athletes with disabilities. Paralympic athletes go through rigorous training year-round to prepare. They are the best in their sports, who, through determination and hard work, have earned the honor of representing their country.

The Paralympic Games provide world-class competition at the highest level, and participants compete for gold, silver and bronze medals against the world's best athletes with disabilities. Don't confuse the Paralympic Games with the Special Olympic World Games. They are totally separate events with different objectives. The Special Olympics emphasize participation by athletes from ages eight to eighty with learning disabilities. All participants are considered winners and receive medals.

The Paralympic Games are the second-largest sporting event in the world behind the Olympics. The Paralympics feature twenty-one sports, eighteen of which are also contested in the Olympics.

Following the theme "Triumph of the Human Spirit," the Paralympic Games is proud of the tradition it has established to bring elite disabled athletic competition to the forefront of public consciousness. Competitive sports have proven to be an effective vehicle to promote equality, inclusion, accessibility, and awareness about the capabilities of those with physical disabilities. Competitive sports dispel the age-old stigma surrounding disabilities and illuminate the realm of possibility. The Paralympics truly signify all that is right in sports.

developed for many mainstream sports as well. Track and field is very big. Many visually impaired kids run on their school track teams. A totally blind runner may use a guide runner. They require two lanes, and the guide runner has a tether. The blind runner sets the pace, and the blind runner has to cross the finish line first. There is a lot of coordination involved, especially coming out of the starting block.

Runners with some vision learn to key on other runners. At a track meet, the high school coach must study the other team and find someone who is about the same speed. Then the visually impaired runner fixes on his unintended guide runner. Visually impaired runners find it easier when they have an outside lane, because the grass line is much easier to see than painted white lines.

Goalball

Jackie Barns, age eighteen, is a high school student with visual impairment and high ambitions. She is a contender for the U.S. Paralympic Goalball Team. Jackie says, "Sports give me something to do other than school and homework. I love to be active and get my mind off of school once in a while. When I'm playing sports, I concentrate only on the game, and not on the problems I've encountered throughout my day or the tests I think I've failed.

"Goalball is a very intense sport, especially at the higher levels. Goalball gives me a chance to compete all out on an equal basis with other people. As far as other sports, I pick the ones that I have the most fun in. Swimming is an all-around good exercise, plus it's good to loosen up all of the muscles that may be sore from goalball or running.

"I've always been interested in soccer, and I used to play on a traveling soccer team. Since I've lost a good part of my

Diving in goalball. Photo by author.

vision I still feel that I have enough to play the game. I already know all the rules and how to play, so now it's just a matter of being really astute to what's happening on the field, whether I listen to what's going on or just see with the little vision I have.

"My vision was just fine up until about eighth grade, when I started losing a lot. I found out I had Stargardt's Disease when I was eight years old, but it didn't actually affect me until later. So I guess I've been visually impaired for about four years now.

"Goalball is my favorite sport because I've met some really cool people along the way, and goalball is never a boring, slow sport. There's always room to improve in goalball. When I'm standing ready to dive, after the people from the other end throw the ball, I'm clueless as to where I'll end up diving. Within the two seconds I have to find out where the ball is going, dive there, and get it. It's definitely a rush, no doubt. When the fast throwers are across from me, I do have some hesitations in throwing myself in front of the ball. Knowing that pain will follow is a hard fear to overcome. A couple years ago when I was starting out with goalball, when I heard that a hard thrower was about to throw, I would just simply not dive for fear of being hurt. But now I overcome that, and with good form, the hit won't hurt as much."[12]

Sixteen-year-old Kathryn Healy agrees. She says, "It was a little intimidating at first. As our team got better, the throws got faster and harder to block. Every good goalball player goes through the fear of the ball, but it's either get down and block the ball or quit the sport. I choose to get down and block the ball.

"It's one of the few team sports that a sighted person and a visually impaired person can play at an equal level. I've brought a few friends along, and everyone has really liked it. Everyone can have fun at once and still be quite serious."[13]

Each year Kathryn and Jackie's team, the Tsunami, travel to Florida to compete in national games. Traveling with blind athletes brings a special set of challenges, says their coach, Jackie Pieper.

GOALBALL

Goalball is the only team sport created for athletes with visual impairments. Because there are different levels of visual impairment, all players wear eye masks that block out all light. It's played on a volleyball-size court that is marked with tape that has string under it, so the players can feel the boundaries. The ball is about the size of a basketball, but it's heavier and is thrown along the floor like a bowling ball—sometimes as fast as forty-five miles per hour. The ball contains several rattles that make a sound like paper clips being tossed in a jar, and that's how players know where it is. Silence is vital, and during the game only the players and referees are allowed to talk. "In the Paralympics in Atlanta, they had several thousand fans, and during timeouts they screamed bloody murder, but they are dead silent during the play. The spectators have to learn to button it up," says Dr. Paul Ponchillia.

There are three players on a team. Teams alternate throwing the ball end to end, and a point is scored when a team gets the ball across its opponent's goal line. Defending players stay close to their own goal line and block the oncoming ball with their bodies by diving to the floor. Players have only ten seconds after the ball has touched them to return it, so it's a fast-paced game. The players wear volleyball knee and elbow pads and hockey hip pads, which are nylon for easy slip and slide.

Robin Theryoung plays on the U.S. Paralympic Goalball Team, which is ranked number one in the world. "To play good goalball," says Theryoung, "you need listening skills to track and localize where the ball is. These are the same skills that people with visual impairments need in everyday life."[14]

Big airports can be confusing enough for sighted travelers, but if you can't read the signs on the wall, the arrival and departure screens, airports are difficult to navigate. If you can't see the small print on your ticket and boarding pass, or the number on the airplane seat, you face even more challenges.

At the hotel, Pieper takes the team members to their rooms.

Marlon Shirley, the world's fastest amputee and Team Ossur member. Courtesy of Ossur.

"I walk into the room and tell them where things are, the remote, the phone. I read them the instructions on how to call my room. Memory is one of those things kids with visual impairment really have to work on. It's their life source."[15]

At the time of this writing, USA Women's Goalball Team is number two in the world and the men's team is number three.

SPORTS SAVED HIS LIFE

Until Dan Ferreria was fifteen, he didn't know about wheelchair sports. Ferreria has osteogenesis imperfecta,

GRANTS FOR ATHLETES WITH DISABILITIES

The Challenged Athletes Foundation (CAF) was created in the belief that people of all abilities should have the opportunity to pursue a life full of physical activity and of sports. Whether their goals are recreational or the pursuit of a gold medal at the Paralympic Games, people with physical disabilities are limited by their access to funding.

As one of the very few charities that provides grants directly to athletes with a physical disability, the CAF has raised more than $6 million dollars and directly assisted sixteen hundred challenged athletes worldwide.

Established in 1997, the CAF recognizes the athletic greatness of people with disabilities and supports these efforts by providing grants for training, competition, and equipment needs. Grants are awarded regardless of a person's type of disability, sport, or level of ability.

Applications are accepted year round and the grants are distributed once a year. Learn more at the CAF website: caf.temp.powweb.com/html/pages/about_caf.

Melissa Mitchell on ski chair. Courtesy of Melissa Mitchell.

commonly called "brittle bones." He recalls, "My freshman year I transferred to a special school called the Massachusetts Hospital School, a residential facility where they had wheelchair sports. It changed my life. I went from being completely negative about my disability to figuring out who I was. Wheelchair sports taught me that I'm a competitive person. I learned that my disability wouldn't hinder me from setting and achieving goals."

Ferreria has gone on to coach college wheelchair basketball and is now youth programmer for the Great Lakes Adaptive Sports Association in Illinois. He says, "The same rules apply in sports and in life. The physical gift is important, but the ability to keep your focus is just as important. You set goals in sports, and it rubs off on the rest of your life."[16]

RESOURCES

The Challenged Athletes Foundation provides grants to athletes with disabilities. www.challengedathletes.org

The National Beep Baseball Association oversees the adaptive version of America's favorite pastime for the blind and visually impaired. www.nbba.org

The National Disability Sports Alliance is the national coordinating body for competitive sports for individuals with cerebral palsy, traumatic brain injuries, and survivors of stroke. It also provides programming for other physically disabling conditions such as muscular dystrophy and multiple sclerosis. www.ndsaonline.org

Quad Rugby Central. At Quad Rugby Central you can follow Team USA, find the closest rugby team to participate in, learn about the game or shop at the Rugby Store. www.quadrugby.com

Sailing Alternatives provides instruction and the opportunity to sail for those affected by disabilities. www.sailingalternatives.org

Sports 'n Spokes magazine is published by the Paralyzed Veterans of America and covers many aspects of wheelchair sports. www.pvamagazines.com/sns

The United States Association of Blind Athletes works to increase the number and quality of grassroots through competitive world-class athletic opportunities for Americans who are blind or visually impaired. www.usaba.org

The U.S. Handcycling Federation supports handcycling, a form of adaptive cycling that enables athletes of all abilities to ride a "bike" exclusively using the upper body. Handcycling is also one of the newest competitions at the Paralympic Games, where it made its first appearance in Athens, Greece, in 2004. www.ushf.org

U.S. Paralympics, a division of the United States Olympic Committee, coordinates the preparation and selection of athletes to U.S. Paralympic Teams, and also works with national and locally focused sport organizations to promote Olympic ideals throughout the American population, especially among those Americans who have physical disabilities. www.usolympicteam.com/paralympics

Wheelchair Sports USA is directed by wheelchair athletes and wheelchair sports enthusiasts. Junior athletes make up 30 percent of the total membership. www.wsusa.org

NOTES

1. Mike Froggly, interview with author, October 27, 2003.
2. Michael Van Cleve, interview with author, October 21, 2003.
3. Carl Hamming, interview with author, October 20, 2003.
4. Mike Froggly, interview with author, October 27, 2003.
5. Matt Scott, interview with author, October 18, 2005.
6. Froggly, interview with author, October 27, 2003.
7. Tracy Chynoweth, interview with author, October 18, 2005.
8. Shawna Culp, interview with author, October 18, 2003.
9. Becki Streit, interview with author, September 22, 2003.
10. Dan Burton, interview with author, September 29, 2005.
11. Dr. Paul Ponchillia, interview with author, October 17, 2003.
12. Jackie Barns, e-mail, September 25, 2003, and October 18, 2003.
13. Kathryn Healy, interview with author, October 18, 2003.
14. Robin Theryoung, interview with author, September 21, 2003.
15. Jackie Pieper, interview with author, October 15, 2003.
16. Dan Ferreria, interview with author, September 26, 2003.

5 Express Yourself

LIGHTS, CAMERA, ACTION!

Film is a mirror of life, and the characters in our favorite sitcom can seem as real as the person sitting next to us in chemistry class. But films can be a reverse fun house mirror, reflecting a world of drop-dead gorgeous people in which none of us would actually feel at home—and how often do our TV pals include anyone with a disability?

Hollywood and television are doing a little better. Jeff Shannon, who writes for *New Mobility Magazine*, quotes Gail Williamson, coordinator of talent development and industry relations in the Hollywood-based Media Access Office, as saying, "For [younger filmmakers] disability is no big deal, and that awareness is increasingly showing itself in student films and beyond."[2]

"Art holds the ability to open people. It provides a medium through which to look at ourselves and to look at our world without feeling threatened, and without passing judgment. Art can help us understand."

—Hanna Miller, 24, is pursuing her Master of Fine Arts degree at the Rhode Island School of Design. She has muscular dystrophy and scoliosis.[1]

Quadriplegic actor Dan Murphy has appeared in the Farrelly brothers' comedies *Kingpin*, *There's Something About Mary*, *Shallow Hal*, and *Me, Myself & Irene*. Actor Daryl "Chill" Mitchell, who was paralyzed in a 2001 motorcycle accident, has led the charge in the NBC television series *Ed*. One *Ed* episode followed Mitchell as he got ready for an ordinary day, showing how much more complicated and time consuming a simple morning routine can be for a person in a wheelchair.

Oscar winner and Deaf-rights activist Marlee Matlin, in her recurring role as a White House polling consultant on the TV drama *The West Wing* and her recent role in the film

INDIVIDUAL CAPTIONING SYSTEM FOR DEAF PLAYGOERS

Until now, the ability to attend live theater has been a challenge for the deaf and hard of hearing, who require signed performances or specific seats to make much sense of the play. Now the I-Caption system by Sound Associates Inc. is changing that.

The I-Caption is the latest innovation in assistive technology. A handheld wireless unit displays dialogue and lyrics in real-time text from any seat in the house. The text is automated and synchronized with sound and lighting cues to match the pacing variations from show to show, and a polarized screen keeps nearby patrons from being distracted by the light.

I-Caption is available for all performances of the multiple Tony Award–winning musical *Wicked*, playing at the Gershwin Theater in New York City, as well as for the national touring company of *Big River*.

"We want to break down the barriers that blind, deaf, hearing impaired, non-English speakers, and senior citizens face daily by providing technology to make their live theatrical experience as comfortable and enjoyable as possible," says Ann Tramon, vice president of the Sound Associates Infrared Division.[3]

What the Bleep Do We Know? has created a persona that is both combative and capable.

Shannon writes in *New Mobility*, "The casual, non-judgmental depiction of disability has grown increasingly common in roles ranging from superheroes to street punks. Patrick Stewart leads the X-Men from his futuristic wheelchair, heroically promoting the acceptance of outcasts; Ricardo Montalban pilots a helicopter wheelchair in *Spy Kids 2: The Island of Lost Dreams* (2002); and in the super-powered thriller *Unbreakable* (2000), Samuel L. Jackson's use of a wheelchair is merely an extension of his intensely enigmatic character.

"On a more earthbound level, rapper/actor Snoop Dogg makes a memorable appearance as a paraplegic in *Training*

Day (2001), and in the recent release *Biker Boyz*, a young black 'para' is openly accepted as one of the 'boyz.' Similar incidental depictions of disability can be found in *Driven* (Burt Reynolds as a para!), *Notting Hill*, *Muriel's Wedding*, and the 2002 indie flick *Cherish*. In each case, disability is merely an accepted fact of life, liberated from the stigma of stereotype."[4]

ACTORS WITH DISABILITIES STILL FACE JOB DISCRIMINATION

Performers with disabilities are significantly underrepresented in the entertainment industry and "often reluctant to ask producers for even the most minor accommodations," according to a 2005 study by the Screen Actors Guild (SAG).

Less than 2 percent of TV show characters display a disability, and only .5 percent have speaking roles, says the group in a press release:

"While more than 33 percent of SAG's performers with disabilities indicate a reasonable accommodation would help them in their work, 60 percent never ask for an accommodation—even one so slight as having a cane nearby or asking a producer to face them when they speak," the study reports. The reason for this was because performers "fear employers would be reluctant to hire them."

"The ADA was a quantum leap in the right direction, and SAG has been a tremendous advocate," said *CSI: Crime Scene Investigation* regular Robert David Hall, who chairs SAG's national Performers with Disabilities Committee. "But today, we have the first real documentation of what performers with disabilities and their advocates have long suspected: we have far to go to achieve true equality of opportunity."

Little data has existed until now on performers with disabilities. The annual Casting Data Report tallies opportunities in film and television by race, ethnicity, gender and age—but not disability. SAG is petitioning the U.S. Labor Department to permit expansion of the report to include annual information on performers with disabilities.

"The images we see, and the stories we tell say a lot about our society," says Hall. "People with disabilities should be part of that story."[5]

Two of the five films nominated for best picture at the 2004 Academy Awards had main characters with a disability. *Ray* is a biography of the world-famous blind musician Ray Charles, and *Million Dollar Baby* is the fictional story of a female boxer who becomes a quadriplegic. The 2005 documentary *Murderball*, nominated for an Oscar in 2006, follows a group of powerful young men, living independent lives, who have turned their lack of traditional mobility into the full-speed-ahead and bruising sport of quadriplegic rugby.

According to Shannon, the best way to improve the way films portray people with disabilities is for more people with

AXIS Dance Company dancers Jacques Judith Smith and Jacques Poulin-Denis. Photo by Margot Hartford.

disabilities to break into Hollywood. He is optimistic. He says, "The ultimate solution—growing numbers of disabled people writing, directing, and acting in films and television—is inevitable. Lacking any cohesive force as a civil rights entity ('Why don't we march on Washington? Because it's a bitch to get there!'), the disabled are empowered by the 1990 passage of the Americans with Disabilities Act, by increasing awareness among the nondisabled, and by their own individual initiative."[6]

EVERYBODY DANCE NOW

When it comes to dancing, wheels can work as well as feet. Just ask the members of the AXIS Dance Company in Oakland, California; Dancing Wheels in Cleveland, Ohio; or Full Radius Dance in Atlanta, Georgia.

"Dance is a way to express myself," says seventeen-year-old Jessie. Jessie was born with cerebral palsy and moves through life in a motorized chair. She has a poster on her wall—a photo of a ballet slippers dangling from the arm of a wheelchair. Big letters spell out, "A whole new spin on dance."

"I like to dance to a lot of different music," Jessie says. "I can make up a whole dance like [*wave of hand*] that."

Jessie and several friends in wheelchairs wanted to join their school's dance company. They were allowed to create their own dance to perform at the dance concert, but couldn't practice with the rest of the troupe because rehearsals were held out of wheelchair access. "They don't have a lift yet," says Jessie. "It's going to take time."[7]

When Jessie dances, her gaze turns inward, and she focuses totally as her arms and neck swing in graceful arches. Twirling her chair, she stretches out straight or draws herself into a small knot in perfect unison with the swells of melody or lyric.

Wheelchair dance companies and classes are cropping up all over the country to feed the powerful urge to dance that is not confined to those in toe shoes. Dancing Wheels has been integrating professional stand-up and sit-down dancers since 1980. Throughout the last two decades, Dancing Wheels has performed for, taught, and inspired children and adults of all abilities around the world. In the United States, the company presents more than one hundred performances reaching audiences of 125,000 each year. AXIS Dance Company has created an exciting body of work developed by dancers with and without disabilities since 1987. Troupes like these are paving the way for a powerful and inclusive dance form called "physically integrated dance."

Wheelchair dancers also compete in their very physical art form in the Paralympics. Athletes with physical disabilities that affect the lower limbs are eligible to participate in wheelchair dance sport. To compete in this sport you need to be able to accelerate and stop your wheelchair with either hand. There are competitions in dances like the waltz, tango, samba, cha-cha, and jive. The competition includes a wheelchair user dancing with a nondisabled partner, two wheelchair users dancing together, or a wheelchair user dancing alone.

Gallaudet Dance Company of Gallaudet University. Photo by Benjamin Baylor.

Just because you can't hear the beat, doesn't mean you can't feel it. The Gallaudet Dance Company celebrated its fiftieth anniversary in 2005. The company has evolved from modern dance with abstract signs to incorporate a wider repertoire of ballet, jazz, hip-hop, tap, and dance incorporated with American Sign Language.

Sharon Davis writes on the Gallaudet University website, "The Gallaudet Dance Company is a performing group of approximately 15 dancers. All members of the company are undergraduate or graduate students at Gallaudet University, the world's only accredited liberal arts university for Deaf and hard of hearing students. Each dancer's background is different—both in terms of hearing loss, preferred communication mode, secondary school education, and current major field of study as a University student. But all the dancers are excellent communicators. They rely on their vision as their primary mode of communication and communicate through their dancing in a range of styles, including dance that uses American Sign Language as its foundation. Gallaudet University itself is a bilingual community where students, faculty, and staff communicate with each other in both American Sign Language and English."[8]

The technique Deaf dancers use create their performances is explained on the Gallaudet University website by Diane Hottendorf and Sue Gill-Doleac. "Many people have the misconception that deaf people 'hear' by feeling vibrations through the floor. How is this possible, especially if a person is moving and jumping so that they do not keep in continuous contact with the floor? What if the floor is not wood, but solid concrete?"[9]

The Gallaudet Dancers need many hours of practice in order to develop the inner sense of timing needed for a specific dance. Some dancers who have residual hearing may pick up cues from the music to assist them in knowing where they are supposed to be in a dance, but this does not happen the first time they learn a new dance; it happens only after countless hours of practice and counting all the movements in a dance step. Whether the dancer can use his or her residual hearing will also depend on his or her type of hearing loss (high- or low-frequency loss) and the music (bass or treble tones). Many Deaf dancers can discriminate bass tones better than treble.

When a dance instructor is teaching a new dance routine to Deaf performers, counting visually helps establish the basic rhythm pattern and facilitates the development of inner rhythm and timing for a particular dance. In addition, when teaching a new dance step, it helps if the instructor gives a sign count for each step, similar to giving a verbal count with hearing dancers. Occasionally, an instructor might use a drum to demonstrate the precise rhythm of a piece of music. Often a Deaf dancer will use his or her eyes to watch and follow the movement of a fellow dancer who may be able to hear and follow the music.

The Gallaudet Dance Company remains "in time" with or without music through the use of the same highly developed sense of timing often found in experienced musicians, especially drummers.

Dancing Wheels Summer Dance Workshops. Photo by Hoang Ngoc Dang, 2005.

ALL WRITE

Do you keep a journal? Have you written a short story or a poem that gets your feelings just right? Or maybe you'd like to try your hand at playwriting. VSA arts, an international nonprofit organization, works to create opportunities in the arts for people with disabilities.

VSA arts was founded in 1974 by Ambassador Jean Kennedy Smith with the goal of creating a society where all people with disabilities learn through, participate in, and enjoy the arts. VSA arts is an affiliate of the John F. Kennedy Center for the Performing Arts.

The VSA arts Playwright Discovery Award program challenges middle and high school students of all abilities to take a closer look at the world around them, examine how disability affects their lives and the lives of others, and express their views through the art of writing a one-act play. The award recipients receive scholarship awards and a trip to Washington, D.C., to see their plays performed at the Kennedy Center. For more information on the Playwright Discovery Award, e-mail info@vsarts.org.

In 2005 sixteen-year-old Phoebe Rush of Highland Park, Illinois, won the competition for her script *3/4 of a Mass for St. Vivian*. Set in the early 1970s, the play focuses on the relationship between Vivian, a teenager with cystic fibrosis, and Emily, a friend struggling to find her own identity.

VSA arts also supports flash fiction and poetry through *Infinite Difference*, an online literary journal showcasing the creative writing of middle and high school students. The journal presents pieces selected by a distinguished panel of professional writers and teachers. The call asks students to "explore the beauty in variety, in perceived imperfections, and in the infinite complexities of 'difference.'" The ten pieces chosen offer diverse interpretations on this theme and best exemplify the creative voices that emerge from experiences with disability.

Infinite Difference also includes poems and creative nonfiction by Ekiwah Adler Beléndez, a gifted young poet from Mexico with cerebral palsy. Ekiwah's work and personal

THE KNOTS OF C.P.

**C.P. binds me in a way
of simple everyday things.
Those binds have little knots
and big knots.
Some knots I can get out,
some knots stay knots,
some are just simply knots
I can't untie.
Loving people ignore those knots
and help me untie them.
Bottom line is, people can see
me in two ways.
With knots.
Or without the knots of C.P.**

**—Hannah Thompson, 16.
Hannah has cerebral palsy.**

story provide a backdrop for the important literary contributions of young people around the world.

Writing is so much more than that five-hundred-word essay due on Friday. People have been writing since they began to smear paint on walls and scratch marks into slabs of mud, and we can still read what they had to say. Let it all out. Tell the world. We need to hear from you, whether you like flash fiction, poetry, articles, playwriting, or screenwriting. You can find lots of forums for your words. E-zines devoted to the perspective of young people with physical disabilities are multiplying, but writing is an art that doesn't discriminate. Write now! Who knows where your words will end up?

HOW CAN I KEEP FROM SINGING?

"I actually enjoy playing clarinet a lot more since losing my vision," says Courtney Glodowski. "I'm not just reading it off a page. I'm playing from my heart. It is a more moving experience. My hearing has increased so much. It's amazing what I can hear. I have really got to the point of picking out certain cars in traffic. I can hear curbs. It's a different kind of echoing. It sounds softer or harder or echoing. It's hard to explain."[10]

Patrick Hughes has played piano concerts around the world. He has performed at the Kennedy Center in Washington, D.C., and at the Grand Ole Opry. He received the 2005 VSA arts Panasonic Young Soloists Award. He's been featured in *People* magazine, speaks fluent Spanish, and has a 3.9 grade-point average at Atherton High School in Kentucky. He has received the Presidential Award for

Patrick Hughes has performed at the John F. Kennedy Center in Washington, D.C., at the Grand Ole Opry. Photo courtesy of Patrick Hughes.

WEBSITE FOR DEAF AND HARD-OF-HEARING ARTISTS

The National Technical Institute for the Deaf has launched a groundbreaking website for Deaf and hard-of-hearing artists. The site is believed to be the largest offered by any college for this underrecognized group of artists. It includes art and biographical information for more than forty professional artists from around the world. Students at NTID and its parent institution, the Rochester Institute of Technology, have also created self-portraits reflecting their experiences of what it means to be deaf.

"These artists are often overlooked and neglected," says Patricia Durr, associate professor in NTID's cultural and creative studies department. "We will be expanding this site periodically. We're discovering new artists and are finally getting responses from some well-known deaf artists."[11]

The website began when two local art teachers saw a need for better research materials on Deaf artists. To explore the site, go to www.rit.edu/deafartists.

Outstanding Academic Achievement from both President Bill Clinton and President George W. Bush.

Patrick was born without eyes, a condition called bilateral anophthalmia, which affects one in every one hundred thousand babies. He also has syndrome pterygium, which is a tightening in the joints of the elbows and knees, which prevents him from straightening his arms and legs and keeps him from walking. Patrick had two titanium rods attached to his spine in 1999 to correct scoliosis caused by spending so much time in a wheelchair.

"Ever since I was little, I've been drawn to music," Patrick says. "My dad studied piano and violin in college. When I would cry at night, he would lay me on the piano and play something. I got quiet, so he assumed I liked it. When I was nine months old, Dad took the tray off the highchair and set me in front of the piano. We started doing listen-and-play. By the age of two, I was playing my nursery rhymes."

A senior in high school, Patrick is trying to decide between two career paths. He would like to be either a country music singer or an international Spanish interpreter. To maintain his excellent grades, Patrick requires a lot of support and a lot of planning ahead.

"There might have been a couple of times when I've asked, 'Why am I blind? Why can't I walk?'" Patrick says. "But I might as well ask 'Why do I play the piano so well?' I've never been angry about my disability. My message to all teens with a disability is: You should never let your disability hamper what you do. You can do anything you set your mind to."[12]

A PICTURE IS WORTH A THOUSAND WORDS

Statia Wilson is an art and journalism major at UW Whitewater. Cerebral palsy has left her with the ability to move only her head very precisely, and she uses that skill to operate the communication device in her laptop with a head stick. She paints in oils. She holds the brush with her head stick. "Typically, someone sets my paints up, and I can change and mix the colors by myself," says Statia. "I love landscapes."[13]

Statia has been painting since she was four. She first started painting with her hand. In second grade, she started using her

Statia Wilson paints in oils. Photo by author.

head stick. She has a table designed to fit her wheelchair set up in her dorm room so she can keep painting after she leaves the studio.

"Statia's work is really good," says her art professor, Sam Norgard. "She really contributes a lot to the class. The expression—the mark she makes. It's powerful."[14]

Angelica Busque recently graduated from the Art Institute of Chicago. Angelica's illustrations can be seen throughout this book. She was awarded third place in Shifting Gears—a national competition of graphic art among young artists with disabilities, sponsored by VSA arts and Volkswagen. Artists were asked to illustrate the theme Shifting Gears, and graphically reflect on a pivotal time in their lives that led them to greater understanding of themselves in relation to art and/or their disability. Fifteen finalists were selected from 215 submissions, and their work has been displayed at the Smithsonian Institution in Washington, D.C.

Angelica has lupus, a disorder of the immune system. Normally the immune system protects the body against invading infections and cancers. In lupus, the immune system is overactive and produces increased amounts of abnormal antibodies that attack the body's tissues and organs. Angelica has had her hip replaced and her spleen removed because of the lupus.

"Art has always been my life," says Angelica. "Art is a way of telling your own story. It's an incredible outlet. It has helped me tell how I see things with a disability. I've started doing a comic book called *Morning Star* that came out of my pre-op and the time I was in the hospital. *Morning Star* was the first thing I've done art-wise for a long time. I didn't do art so much when I was sick. Those fifty-six pages were a major accomplishment.

"Being in Chicago introduced me to different comic book artists and their styles. My style is based on journal and diary entries. I turn them into a story. It's almost filmlike. I want to do more graphic novels. Each time you draw something, you get better and better. I feel I can be much more."[15]

"Everyone deserves an opportunity to experience the arts," says Stephanie Moore, director of visual arts for VSA arts. "The arts are a valuable tool that can open doors, incite dreams, and build bridges. We cannot omit people with disabilities from this forum.

"We have three programs geared toward artists between the ages of sixteen and twenty-five: the Volkswagen program, performing arts through the Kennedy Center, and a playwriting program. VSA arts has programs for artists who

© 2002 Sunaura Taylor, "Vic Chesnutt," oil on canvas (6 ft. × 4 ft.) This painting was a recent finalist in Shifting Gears, sponsored by VSA arts and Volkswagen of America, a juried exhibit of award-winning young artists with disabilities.

are trying to become established in their careers, and we work to integrate arts into the lives of kids with disabilities in the school systems. We have affiliates in fifty states and sixty-four countries."[16]

Isaac Powell was awarded the Grand Prize in a recent Shifting Gears juried exhibition. Isaac was born without a right hand. "I've always loved to draw," Isaac says. "In college I was drawn to forestry. I loved the beauty, but that field turned out to be more business-oriented than I had hoped. I was more interested in the aesthetic aspects of forestry. After my freshman year, I decided to go after what I've always loved—drawing. I'm still in school, so I don't know if I'll be able to support myself.

"At first, my work didn't revolve around my disability at all. I tried to steer far away from that because I felt if I painted images of hands or prosthetics that I would be relying on my disability as a crutch. It would be easy to talk about the loss of a hand, but I didn't want to go the easy way.

"Then I decided I would paint hands and prosthetics and very personal imagery. I tried to approach it in an in-your-face mode. After that, I wanted to be more thoughtful. I decided to create icons for myself. For instance, a leaf would be an icon for the hand. Limbs of trees and leaves are the hands. These are icons that I understand, but the viewer doesn't have to get hit over the head. That's where I am now."[17]

RESOURCES

Axis Dance is a California dance company renowned for creating and presenting high-quality contemporary dance by dancers with and without disabilities. www.axisdance.org

The California Governor's Committee on Employment of People with Disabilities has created a Media Access Office to actively promote the employment and accurate portrayal of persons with disabilities in all areas of the media and entertainment industry. www.disabilityemployment.org/med_acc.htm

Dancing Wheels is one of the country's premier integrated dance companies. www.gggreg.com/dancingwheels.htm

Disability Sports regulates wheelchair dance sport for the Paralympics. edweb6.educ.msu.edu/kin866/spwheelchairdance.htm

Films Involving Disabilities presents a detailed list of twenty-five hundred feature films that involve various disabilities. It is directed toward teachers, students, and anyone who has an interest in how disability is represented in films. www.disabilityfilms.co.uk

The Gallaudet Dance Company website explains techniques for Deaf and hard-of-hearing dancers. depts.gallaudet.edu/dance/techniques.html

Lefens, Tim. *Flying Colors: The Story of a Remarkable Group of Artists and the Transcendent Power of Art.* Boston: Beacon Press, 2002.

Murderball. This is the website for *Murderball*, quite possibly the best film ever made about people with disabilities. www.murderballmovie.com/about.html

The National Technical Institute for the Deaf has launched a great website for Deaf and hard-of-hearing artists. www.rit.edu/deafartists

VSA arts is an international nonprofit organization that works to create a society where people with disabilities can learn through, participate in, and enjoy the arts. Currently 5 million people participate in VSA arts programs every year through a network of affiliates nationwide and in more than sixty countries. www.vsarts.org.

World Around You lets you explore the world of Deaf culture, news, and stories from the United States and around the world. clerccenter.gallaudet.edu/WorldAroundYou/index.html

NOTES

1. Hannah Miller, Award of Excellence winner in "Shifting Gears," a juried exhibit of fifteen award-winning young artists with disabilities, www.vsarts.org/prebuilt/showcase/gallery/exhibits/vw/2005/artists/h_miller.html.

2. Jeff Shannon, "Access Hollywood: Disability in Recent Films and Television," *New Mobility*, May 2003, newmobility.com/review_article.cfm?id=690&action=browse (January 30, 2006).

3. Dennis van der Heijden, "ICaption makes All Performances in theater Accessible to the Deaf and Hard of Hearing," Assistive Technology News Portal, August 26, 2005, www.axistive.com/6021/icaption-makes-all-performances-in-theater-accessible-to-the-deaf-and-hard-of-hearing.html (October 19, 2006).

4. Shannon, "Access Hollywood."

5. Screen Actors Guild, "SAG Releases Groundbreaking Report on Performers with Disabilities to Mark 15th Anniversary of Americans with Disabilities Act," July 26, 2005, www.sag.org/sagWebApp/application?origin=news_and_events_archives.jsp&event=bea.portal.framework.internal.refresh&pageid=Hidden&contentUrl=/templates/newsLander.jsp&newsUrl=/Content/Public/pwd_pressrelease-7-25-05.htm&cp=NewsAndEventsArchives (October 19, 2006).

6. Shannon "Access Hollywood."

7. Jessie Martin, interview with author, September 18, 2003.

8. Gallaudet University, "The Gallaudet Dance Company," depts.gallaudet.edu/dance/dancers.html (August 31, 2005).

9. Diane Hottendorf and Sue Gill-Doleac, "Dance Techniques for Deaf and Hard of Hearing Dancers," Gallaudet University website, depts.gallaudet.edu/dance/techniques.html (August 31, 2005).

10. Courtney Glodowski, interview with author, June 29, 2005.

11. "NTID Creates Web Gallery for Deaf Artists," *Rochester Democrat and Chronicle*, October 14, 2005, www.ntid.rit.edu/media/full_text.php?article_id=440 (October 19, 2006).

12. Patrick Hughes, interview with author, August 17, 2005.

13. Statia Wilson, interview with author, October 18, 2005.

14. Sam Norgard, interview with author, October 14, 2005.

15. Angelica Busque, interview with author, September 6, 2005.

16. Stephanie Moore, e-mail, October 24, 2005.

17. Isaac Powell, interview with author, October 25, 2005.

Relationships

Everyone always makes such a big deal about how teens want to fit in. But teens aren't the only ones. The fact is, though most people get more self-confident as they get older, everyone wants to fit in, and everyone fears that they don't—even the class valedictorian, the star quarterback, and the prom queen.

"Normal is just a setting on the washing machine."
—Mike Hineberg, attendant referral coordinator, IndependenceFirst[1]

FIRST IMPRESSIONS

People with disabilities have an extra challenge when it comes to feeling normal. If you have a wheelchair, a white cane, or even a tiny hearing device tucked discreetly behind your ear, you *know* that's the first thing people notice about you. You may not always be right about that—but often you are.

"That's the curse of being disabled," says Shawna Culp, a cancer survivor. "In wheelchairs, if you come into a room, you know you automatically get looks. My new leg looks more like a real leg. Now I can wear knee socks, and they'll stay up. If I wear pants, people just wonder why I limp."[2]

"I'm a little paranoid about my speech," says Michelle Maloney, who has severe hearing loss in her right ear and moderate hearing loss in her left. "When I came to college, there were people who would comment on my speech. The only thing wrong with my speech is my *s*'s. Unfortunately, that's one of the most common letters in the English language. I get really self-conscious about it. I always ask,

Mich Gerson (right) with her friends Lauren and Steph. Photo courtesy of Mich Gerson.

'How did you find out that I'm hearing impaired?' and that's the main way."[3]

"Usually, when I first meet people, I don't let them know right away that I'm visually impaired," says Kathryn Healy, who has albinism. "I let them find out later because I don't think it's that much of who I am."[4]

FEELING OUT OF IT

According to the National Organization on Disability, people with disabilities spend significantly less time interacting outside the home, socializing, and going out than people without disabilities. They may tend to feel more isolated and participate in fewer activities than their nondisabled counterparts. If you have a disability, it can be harder to build a network of friends with whom you can share your feelings, opinions, and ideas. You may feel that your disability is making others shy away. You might have extra issues with transportation and feel reluctant to venture out. You are not alone.

Statia Wilson with her service dog, Ice Cream.
Photo by author.

"Open lunch—the whole junior and senior class have cars and they leave," says Jessie Martin. Her high school's policy of letting juniors and seniors leave school for lunch has become a daily reminder of the ways in which her wheelchair sets her apart from her friends. "Now I'm a junior, and everyone I know is gone. Even if you have nowhere to go—you go home. You go anywhere to be out of the building at lunch. At 10 at night and 7 in the morning I'm on the phone, calling people to hang out at school. But once people have their ID stamped for open lunch, it's, 'Sorry, Jess. I have plans.'"[5]

"I found my two best friends in college," says Mich Gerson, who is deaf. "Those girls are my backbone—the ones that get me through the really rough times here (and trust me—I've had plenty). I also have an amazing group of friends—God knows I wouldn't be able to get through college without them. I've had too many laughs, too many inside jokes, too many late nights, and so many moments with so many of them that I wouldn't give it up for anything. These friends are all also deaf."[6]

Students sign together at the National Technical Institute for the Deaf. Photo courtesy of the National Technical Institute for the Deaf at Rochester Institute of Technology.

Courtney Glodowski was blinded by an accidental gunshot just before she began high school. "One of the things that surprised me most was how my friends reacted," she recalls. "They were there for me at first. They would come and visit me in the hospital. They helped me around school for a couple of months, and then they started to pretend that I didn't exist.

"They just didn't want to deal with me. I don't think they wanted to take the extra time to come around and describe what was going on for me. It's not that they were doing mean things to me. They were just excluding me. I would sit at the table at lunch with them, and they would be making plans to go to a hockey game. They would all invite each other to go, and no one would invite me, and the next day they would talk about how much fun it was. They didn't even think that I was listening, and it really hurt."[7]

Laura Glowacki had similar experiences as the only blind student in her high school. When she was a sophomore, she left home to attend her state's school for the blind, where her

THE BOND WITH SERVICE DOGS

Quinn Haberl worked hard to get his dog, and Coda works hard for him. Their bond is deep. One of the few places Coda has not been able to accompany Quinn was into the operating room when Quinn had surgery on his cornea. He had twelve stitches in his eyeball. The pain was terrible. Coda cried the entire three hours he was in surgery. She paced the floor, whining softly. Finally, when the gurney was rolled through the doors and Quinn was in it, Coda started to wag her tail. When the nurses left, she put two paws on the bed. Then, and only then, she laid down to rest.

classmates were more accepting. "It's not like I'm the horrible loner who had no friends," she says, "but I didn't have the chance to go out and do things like go to the mall or go roller skating."

"Why do they ignore us?" Laura insightfully answers this question: "They don't know how to act around someone who is different from them. They don't like to feel unsure, so they choose not to associate. They know where their safety and comfort zones are, and they like to stay there. Someone different encroaches on that."[8]

GETTING INTO IT

Other people have had more positive experiences. A good way to build a bridge is to think about what floats your boat and go after it. Develop hobbies. Pursue special interests. Not only will you dig into something you love, but shared interests are a great way to bring people together and develop friendships. Check out the Scouts, a local 4-H Club, a church group,

Angela Kuemell and Alex McKenzie, good friends and counselors at Camp Waubeek, coordinate plans for camp activities. Photo by author.

activities through the parks and recreation department, local community centers, or the YMCA. You never know what you'll find. The more interests you have, the smaller a role your disability will play in how you see yourself—and how others see you.

"Most of the people I deal with—all my friends—are pretty open about different lifestyles," says college junior Alex McKenzie, who has been in a wheelchair since age four. "People don't seem to react to my being in a wheelchair."[9]

Isaac was born without a right hand. "Initially people will treat me differently," he says. "I played sports in high school, and for some reason people respected that. The way I perceive myself—I don't have a disability. I can do just about everything. I may just do it in a different way. Sometimes you're stereotyped, and you need to deal with that."[10]

PROTECTING YOURSELF FROM ABUSE

The isolation and dependence inherent in many forms of disability put you at especially high risk of abuse. If you have to depend on others to meet some or all of your basic needs, care providers have to be involved in close, frequent contact in the most intimate and personal parts of you life. That can increase the opportunity for sexual or other abusive acts. For example, if you are blind, it is difficult to be fully aware of your surroundings, especially on public transportation or out in the community, and that can make you vulnerable to exploitation by others.

"I got really scared one time," says one high school girl with cerebral palsy. "Someone tried to pull me out of my wheelchair and touch me. I was talking to someone, and once he got me out, he tried to touch me in places that I didn't appreciate. He was invading my personal space."

According to United Cerebral Palsy of Michigan, both men and women with disabilities are at least twice as likely

TIPS FOR COMMUNICATING WITH SOMEONE WITH MOBILITY IMPAIRMENTS

- **If possible, put yourself at the wheelchair user's eye level.**
- **Don't lean on a wheelchair or any other assistive device.**
- **Never patronize people who use wheelchairs by patting them on the head or shoulder.**
- **Offer assistance *if* the individual appears to be having difficulty opening a door.**
- **If you phone someone who uses a wheelchair, let the phone ring longer than usual so he or she can get to the phone.**

than their nondisabled counterparts to be victims of violence. Young people with disabilities may experience violence or abuse at home, in school, on the bus, or in a group home.

Karen McCulloh of the National Organization of Nurses with Disabilities agrees that teens with disabilities need to be assertive about their comfort zone. "Nobody has the right to touch you unless you want them to," she says. "If people are touching you in a way that makes you uncomfortable, you have to say something. You have to be able to set boundaries. Make your wishes clear, and if necessary, tell a trusted adult."[11]

DATING

Thinking about and being in relationships occupies a large part of most people's minds. Everyone worries about whether or not they are attractive. Everybody worries about making an idiot of themselves on a date. Most successful relationships are more about affection, caring, respect, and trust, and every successful relationship is based on compromise.

Don't ever believe that no one will love you because you have a disability. The world is full of people with disabilities who both love and are loved. One of the best ways to find the person for you is to get involved in as many activities as you can. When you are out there pursuing your passions, you will meet other people with whom you will connect.

"I've dated girls in wheelchairs and not in wheelchairs," says Alex. "It doesn't really matter. I don't care. It's more about the person—not the chair."[12]

"My fiancé doesn't have a problem that I am blind," says Courtney. "It doesn't bother him that we can't do some things that sighted kids would do, like play basketball. He doesn't feel like he's missing out on anything. We go to movies, and he describes them for me. He does so well with describing, it blows me away."[13]

Michelle, who is now in college, finds her hearing loss can interfere as she tries to reach out and connect. "In a group, I can't hear what everyone is saying," she says. "This is bad, but sometimes I just do the nod-and-smile thing. There can be a lot of interfering noise at parties. Sometimes when a guy is talking to me, I have to try to guess what to say. My friends can sometimes help me. They pick up on what I'm thinking, and they will ask questions to help me understand.

"Now that I'm going to bars, that's a horrible way to get to know someone because it's so loud. Here is my embarrassing story. This summer I met this guy through a friend, and she introduced us, and I thought his name was Todd. He asked me out on a date, and we called each other for a while. About a month later I ran into him when I was out with some friends, and I introduced him as Todd. At the end of the night, he got mad and said, 'My name's not Todd, it's Ty.'

"I felt really stupid. I just wanted to disappear. My friends never once corrected me. He never said anything. Obviously,

TIPS FOR COMMUNICATING WITH SOMEONE WHO IS HARD OF HEARING

- **Get the person's attention before starting to talk. You may tap him or her gently on the shoulder or arm.**
- **Look directly at the person. Keep your face in the light. Speak clearly in a normal tone of voice. Use short, simple sentences. Don't chew gum.**
- **If the person uses a sign language interpreter, speak to the person—not the interpreter.**
- **If you are phoning someone who is hard of hearing, let the phone ring longer than usual. Speak clearly and be prepared to repeat the reason for the call and who you are.**
- **If you don't have a text telephone (TTY), dial 711 to reach the national telecommunications relay service, which will facilitate the call between you and any person who uses a TTY.**

WHY DOES ASL BECOME A FIRST LANGUAGE FOR MANY DEAF PEOPLE?

Children often get their first language skills from their parents, according to the National Institute on Deafness and Other Communication Disorders. A Deaf child who is born to Deaf parents who already use ASL will begin to acquire ASL as naturally as a hearing child picks up spoken language from hearing parents. However, nine out of every ten children who are born deaf are born to parents who hear, and language is acquired differently by Deaf children with hearing parents who have no prior experience with ASL. Some hearing parents choose to introduce sign language to their Deaf children. Hearing parents who choose to learn sign language often learn it along with their children. As with any language, interaction with other children and adults also helps a child to learn sign language.

nothing developed between us. I'm not sure if it was because of that. I double-check names now."[14]

Shawna lost her leg to cancer when she was ten. She uses a prosthetic leg and sometimes a wheelchair. "I think boys are intimidated by it," she says, "but if they are in a group with me or hear me talking to other people, they realize I'm a great person, and have great qualities.

"Now that we can drive, I go out with my friends, and we have fun. We have a lot of guy friends. They are just not people we are interested in relationship-wise. I'm not really

TIPS FOR COMMUNICATING WITH SOMEONE WHO IS BLIND

- **Speak to the person as you approach.**
- **State clearly who you are in a normal tone of voice.**
- **Never touch or distract a service dog without first asking the owner.**
- **Tell the person when you are leaving.**
- **Don't try to lead a blind person without asking first. Let him or her hold your arm and control his or her own movements.**
- **Be descriptive when giving directions.**

interested in dating the boys I know. Not dating now doesn't bother me. I'm really busy with basketball and school. My goals right now are to play basketball in the Paralympics and go to a good college. I know when I get to college, dating is not going to be a problem."[15]

"I've only dated four guys," says Laura, who is now enrolled in a public college. "They were all pretty long-term relationships. All my boyfriends have been visually impaired. I have mixed feelings about that. I met my first boyfriend at blind camp when I was thirteen. We dated forever, like two and a half years. The next two went to school with me, and I dated them each for about a year. It was kind of weird. There were only about sixty of us at school, and we lived in small dorms and ate together every day. It was almost like dating your brother because we know each other so well, but the bonding is so cool.

"I know I am definitely more comfortable with visually impaired people. I know they understand the little aspects of it. I was hoping to get into more casual dating in college, but now I'm going with Mike. He's also blind, but that's cool. We

TIPS FOR COMMUNICATING WITH SOMEONE WITH A SPEECH IMPAIRMENT

- **If you do not understand something the person says, do not pretend you do. Ask the person to repeat what he or she said and then repeat it back.**
- **Be patient. Take as much time as necessary.**
- **Try to ask questions that require only short answers or a nod of the head.**
- **Concentrate on what the person is saying.**
- **Don't speak for the person or attempt to finish his or her sentences.**

are both music majors, and we have a lot more than just visual impairment in common. If I would meet someone open-minded enough to date me, I would be open to the idea of dating someone sighted. It would be fun to have a car to go places in with someone, but really personality is so much more important."[16]

"I've dated both hearing and Deaf guys," says Mich, a student at NITD/RIT. "It's been a tough road for me. I have a very 'hearing' sense of humor. I write and talk like I'm 'hearing,' and it's rare to find a Deaf guy who shares those qualities and be able to click with him. While my speech is relatively comprehensible, hearing people sometimes have to focus when listening to me speak, and not all of them make the effort. This applies to hearing guys. With many of them, I feel I could reach a whole different plateau in my relationship with them, but because of the communication barrier, it becomes difficult.

"With Deaf guys, it's a bit more tricky. Educational background varies throughout the community here. Some didn't have the greatest education, while some went to the 'right' schools and were educated among the best and the brightest. But the thing is, communication is never an issue with any Deaf person. I could go up to any Deaf student here and strike up a conversation in sign language, but in terms of having a heated political discussion on whether stem cell research should be allowed—well, it's not exactly a lot of Deaf people's topic of choice.

"Hearing friends? I have one close hearing friend—Matt. I love Matt. We share the exact same sarcastic sense of humor—a sense of humor that I think is hard to find in the Deaf community. He's also intelligent, articulate, and just a great soul. Matt and I communicate mainly by speaking, but he attends No Voice Zone (a weekly event on campus from 10–11 p.m., where Deaf students and hearing students meet. The Deaf students teach hearing students to sign). Matt is picking up sign fairly quickly."[17]

Nineteen-year-old Matt Shand provides his own perspective on his relationship with Mich: "She is the first

Deaf person I'd ever communicated with. At first, I was pretty nervous and a little intimidated. I met Mich on a website called facebook.com. You basically make a profile and upload your picture, then anyone on your college campus can send you a message, and you can also get in touch with people from other colleges. Mich and I talked on AIM for about a month before we started to hang out.

"Mich is very good at lip reading, so while we couldn't communicate too in-depth in person, she could still understand what I was saying, and I could understand mostly everything she was saying.

"Mich is a really great person to talk to, so our friendship grew, and I became determined to learn sign language so we could communicate more effectively, or at least more comfortably for her. A lot of hearing kids at RIT think that the Deaf students should make more of an attempt to be

Katy Sandberg and Statia Wilson, college classmates and good friends. Photo by author.

friendly, but I think they don't understand that not all Deaf people can read lips or speak easily. I think there should be some initiative taken by hearing kids to learn at least the American Sign Language ABCs. They're really simple, as are most of the signs I've learned from attending No Voice Zone.

"No Voice Zone is wonderful. Groups form based on your experience level with ASL. Level 1 groups work on the ABCs and numbers. Level 2 kids know their letters and a smattering of signs. Level 3 kids are the most advanced. They still want to learn more, or just come for a good time. I've picked up the ABCs really easily, and from there I've been trying to learn signs that are effective in everyday conversation. My apartment mates go to No Voice Zone with me, so it's a good time. Afterwards, we usually invite people back to our apartment to just hang out and talk in ASL.

"Having been friends with Mich for a while now, it's hard for me to remember what it was like when it used to be awkward and a little confusing for us to try to talk in person. Now it's nearly seamless, and if she doesn't understand what I'm saying, I can fingerspell it out without a second thought. If anything, I think our relationship is a deeper one than I have had with many hearing girls. The Deaf people I've met seem a lot more expressive. Emotion is a big part of their communication process, and with that comes empathy and understanding. I've met a lot of Mich's friends, and we all hang out and have a good time and understand each other well enough for conversation to flow smoothly.

"Any relationships are all about compromise. It takes exactly that for hearing and nonhearing kids to communicate, be it learning some sign, learning to read lips or speak. Most find, it's a lot easier to learn sign, and it's fun too."[18]

Making new friends can be scary. Dating is a minefield that we all have to pick our way through. Your disability may seem like a hurdle too high to get in the game, but it is not. Remember that other people are every bit as unsure as you are. Be a good listener and a good companion. Share activities and ideas. Build trust and respect between you and another person. You'll be creating an environment where love can grow.

SEXUALITY

"People are prejudiced about dating among teens with disabilities," says high school teacher Amy Talkowski. "They say 'Isn't that cute?' if they see kids holding hands, but if it gets more serious, those same people get uncomfortable."[19] People with disabilities have to contend with stereotypes that paint them as helpless and sexless. Nothing could be further from the truth.

Don't rush—or be rushed—into sex. Be patient. Relationships take time to develop, and as the Supremes said so long ago, "You can't hurry love." Don't settle for the first person who expresses an interest in you as a woman or a man, unless you are also interested in that person. Find the person who appreciates you for who you are—disability included. That person is out there!

It may feel uncomfortable to talk to someone you are attracted to about your disability. The other person may feel uncomfortable too. Don't be afraid to bring it up yourself, especially if you are developing a relationship with a nondisabled person. Be positive and matter-of-fact. The best relationships are based on truth, trust, and sharing.

Regardless of your disability, lovemaking is doable. Some techniques may be impossible for you, but between loving and trusting partners, mutual pleasure and fulfillment are possible. You will probably need to be creative and flexible and come up with your own signature techniques.

Before you become sexually active, you need to put sex into your own context of values and morals. You also need to know how to protect yourself against unwanted pregnancy, sexually transmitted diseases, and sexual exploitation.

The resources section at the end of this chapter can help you find loads of information on sexuality and disability.

RESOURCES

American Sign Language (ASL) Fingerspelling. This is a very animated website for learning fingerspelling. asl.ms/

The Center for Research on Women with Disabilities (CROWD) at Baylor College of Medicine. This site focuses on health, self-esteem, sexuality, relationships, and disability-related abuse. www.bcm.tmc.edu/crowd

In the Mix, What's Normal? Overcoming Obstacles and Stereotypes. This site is a roadmap on how to overcome obstacles and stereotypes, based on the public television series *In the Mix*. www.pbs.org/inthemix/shows/show_whatsnormal2.html

Sex, Etc. An award-winning website for teens by teens developed by the Center for Applied Psychology at Rutgers, the State University of New Jersey. www.sexetc.org

Voigt, Cynthia. *Izzy, Willy-Nilly*. New York: Atheneum, 1986. After a car accident leaves Izzy disabled, she's determined not to show how much she's hurting. It takes Rosamund, a girl who seems to care nothing about good manners, to help her face her changed existence.

NOTES

1. Michael Hineberg, interview with author, October 20, 2005.
2. Shawna Culp, interview with author, October 18, 2003.
3. Michelle Maloney, interview with author, October 4, 1005.
4. Kathryn Healy, interview with author, October 18, 2003.
5. Jessie Martin, interview with author, April 12, 2005.
6. Mich Gerson, e-mail, October 12, 2005.
7. Courtney Glodowski, interview with author, October 11, 2005.
8. Laura Glowacki, interview with author, September 1, 2005.
9. Alex McKenzie, interview with author, August 26, 2005.
10. Isaac Powell, interview with author, October 25, 2005.
11. Karen McCulloh, interview with author, August 12, 2005.
12. Alex McKenzie, interview with author, August 26, 2005.
13. Glodowski, interview with author, October 11, 2005.
14. Maloney, interview with author, October 4, 1005.
15. Culp, interview with author, October 18, 2003.
16. Glowacki, interview with author, September 1, 2005.
17. Gerson, e-mail, October 12, 2005.
18. Matt Shand, e-mail, October 15, 2005.
19. Amy Talkowski, interview with author, April 12, 2005.

7 Declaring Independence

Everyone has the right to live as independently as they can, regardless of a disability. As you become an adult, you have the right to make your own choices, manage your own affairs, and be a participating member of your community. Independent living doesn't mean you must do everything on your own. You may need help with different activities of daily living. But you will need to develop the skills needed to control your daily life: how to manage your time, how to be a renter and establish a good relationship with your landlord, how to make a budget. Independent living centers are an excellent resource for this valuable info. You will need to learn how to find the right resources in your community, how to contact them, and how to factor the reality of waiting lists into your moving plans.

"Living on your own is the ultimate goal."

—Angela Kuemmel, 23, is pursuing a Ph.D. in psychological studies. A diving accident paralyzed her from the chest down at age 15.[1]

GAINING SKILLS FOR INDEPENDENT LIVING

Each state has centers for independent living. The MetroWest Center for Independent Living in Framingham, Massachusetts, has a cool directory feature on its website at www.virtualcil.net/cils. You can click on your state and find the center closest to you. These centers will provide four core services: advocacy, peer mentoring, independent living skills training, and information and referral. They can help you figure out how to find and apartment and organize it, how to shop, or how to look for work.

According to Michael Hineberg, attendant referral coordinator for IndependenceFirst in Milwaukee, Wisconsin, "No one is completely independent. Every living thing depends on some other living thing for its survival. No one is self-sufficient. The mechanic must go see the doctor, and the doctor must go to the mechanic, and they both need the farmer. Independence is asking for help with tasks that you cannot do by yourself. True independence is maximizing your ability to make your own choices and doing what you can for yourself. It is knowing where and when to go for help. Independence is not so much what you can do, but rather what you do with what you can do."[2]

NATIONAL STUDY OF TRANSITION

The U.S. Department of Education began a study in 2001 of twelve thousand students nationwide who were between the ages of thirteen and sixteen at the start of the study. Information from parents, students, and schools will be collected over ten years. This will give us a national picture of the experiences and achievements of young people with disabilities as they transition into early adulthood.

Building lab skills. Photo courtesy of the National Technical Institute for the Deaf at Rochester Institute of Technology.

The Center for Independent Living in Berkeley, California, is a national leader in helping people with disabilities live independently and become productive, fully participating members of society. Many of the staff members have disabilities, and they are strongly committed to supporting others in their efforts toward self-sufficiency.

Luciana Sandobal, peer counselor and transition advocate at the center, shares both her personal experience and her expertise about programs and services available to help people make the transition to independent living. "We had a kid come in with spina bifida, and he didn't have any services," she says. "He was eighteen, and he didn't know what to do next. He wanted to be more independent in transportation.

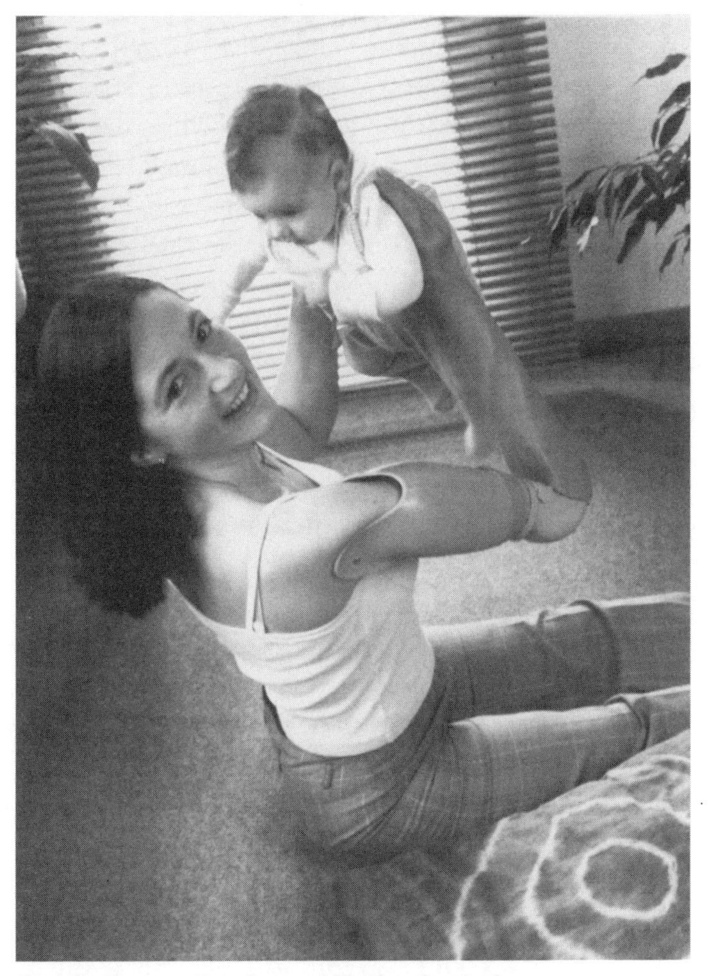

Prosthetic arm. Courtesy of Motion Control.

We showed him the public transportation around here and how he could access the buses with his wheelchair. We had another client; he wouldn't come out of his house. He had a new disability, and he wasn't aware of what he could do. We introduced him to our Moving On Program, where they teach independent living skills. They coached him on how to do laundry, cook, and other basic skills. Now he is living in an apartment by himself and doing really well."[3]

Courtney Glodowski became blind after a shooting accident. "I spent six weeks in the hospital, and I'm still readjusting in different areas. It's everything—like even picking out clothes. I have my hard days and my good days.

"I spend a day and a half each week learning living skills and how to manage a household. I can cook dinners. It's all by touch, feel, and sound. You can hear when water is at a half or full boil. You use timers a lot to keep track of what stage your food is at. Because I could see before, I can envision things in my mind. Last Tuesday, I made homemade chicken noodle soup. I cut up carrots and onion, and boiled chicken to make the broth. Then I took the chicken out and cut it off the bone. I've made peanut butter cookies too.

"I have mobility lessons where I learn to walk around town and get to my classroom, and the department store, and the grocery store. I'm learning what to do if I get lost. I use environmental clues—like how to use the sun for direction. I know where the sun is at different times of the day and year, and I can get my line of direction that way. Maybe there is a busy highway I can hear in the distance. I know it is to the north, and I keep my direction.

"I use a white cane. It tells me what's in front of me, and it lets me know when there are curbs. My hearing has increased so much. It's amazing what I can hear. I have really got to the point of picking out certain cars in traffic. I can hear the echo from curbs. Remembering is important in everything: how many doors down to the left your classroom is, or the order of cereal in the cupboard.

"After losing my vision, I started learning Braille right away. I learned it in about six months. I take notes with electronic Braille. I use it every day in all my classes. I use it in my address book, my planner, my calculator—pretty much everything.

"Next year, I'm going to study court reporting and broadcast captioning at technical college. The opportunities are endless. There are so many different things you can do, and there is a shortage. It's an in-demand job."[4]

Dave Groesbeck, age twenty-two, is living independently, working, and loving it all. Dave lives on the first floor of a new four-unit apartment just a block from a big park. His bedroom is overflowing with NASCAR model cars and plastered with racing posters. Dave has spina bifida.

"It was a long process," he says. "I got hooked up with the county, and they hooked me up with Creative Community Living Services (CCLS). We finally got this apartment approved. They connected me with my roommate, and they hired the staff.

"We have a really nice landlord. The back patio was a little small for our chairs, so he added six more inches to the patio with wood. I always come in through the garage, and he built a ramp there.

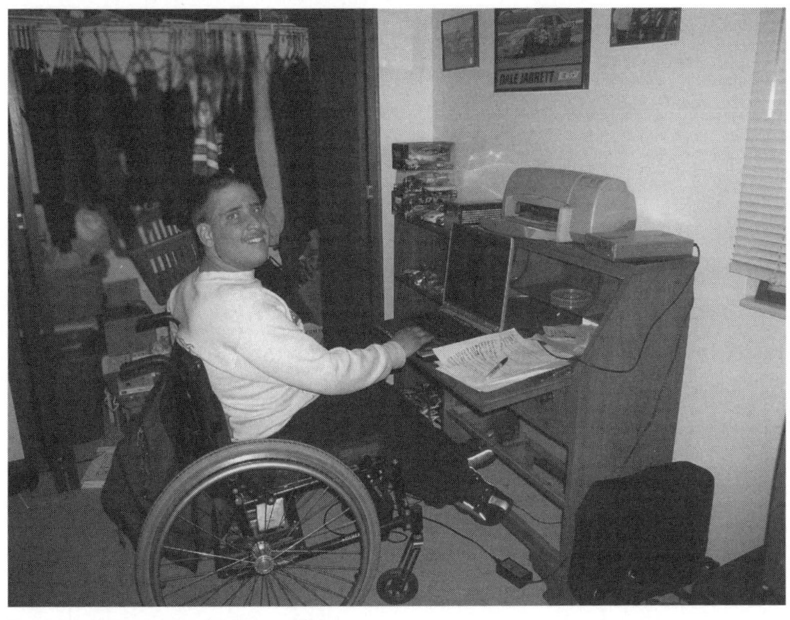

Dave's place. Photo by author.

"Being on my own is different. Sometimes it is a lot to keep track of. Because of my memory, I need someone to be here 24/7. Luckily, I get along with my staff. They are great.

"I work at Valley Packaging Industries. In high school I loved shop. That's why I am doing what I am doing at work. I like building things. But I am currently looking for another assembly job. Now I get paid by the piece. I would like to get paid hourly, or I would like to get fast enough to make at least minimum wage."[5]

Katy Sandberg has cerebral palsy and gets around in her power chair. She had to take charge of her life for the first time when she went to college in a different state: "The hardest thing for me was the whole live-in-aide situation. Before I came here, I wasn't into doing stuff for myself. At camp during the summer, my counselors, who are also in chairs, made me try. I would say 'No, I can't. I've never done it before.' But they encouraged me to do everything for myself. It was a lot of hard work and a lot of tears, but now I encourage other people to take charge too."[6]

Angela Kuemmel credits her independence to the physical therapy team that worked with her after she became paralyzed from the shoulders down by a diving accident at age fifteen. "You are talking about a totally able-bodied teenager," she says. "When I was little, I was the child who would run from my mother in a store without taking a second thought. I was oldest child, doing everything myself. Suddenly I needed help with everything. I needed help being fed. I couldn't dress myself, and I couldn't shower myself. I had three months of inpatient and six months of outpatient rehab. The occupational therapists and physical therapists were very encouraging of independence. They really worked with me to problem solve.

"After a spinal cord injury, they tell you, 'You are going to be independent!' When I came to camp, I met kids who had always had their disability. They haven't always been exposed to independence.

"Independent living—that's the big thing. There are different degrees of independent living and everyone can meet it to some degree.

"Now I'm in graduate school. Finding an apartment in Florida was a nightmare. I had gotten an apartment guide from Forrent.com. I was calling up places to find an apartment. I looked at ten apartments that people had told me were wheelchair accessible, but there was only one I could live in. Everyone has their own definition of wheelchair accessibility. There is a big difference between wheelchair accessible and barrier free. Sure, maybe you can get through the door—but can you use the bathroom and the shower?"[7]

HOME, ACCESSIBLE HOME

There are more and more homes that are both accessible and barrier free thanks to a movement called universal design. The Center for Universal Design was established in 1989 under a grant from the National Institute on Disability and Rehabilitation Research (NIDRR) with a mission to improve the quality and availability of housing for people with disabilities. According to Ron Mace, founder of the Center for Universal Design, "Universal design is the design of products and environments to be usable by all people to the greatest extent possible, without the need for adaptation or specialized design." Things like wider doorways and electrical outlets placed two or more feet above the floor are starting to find their way into many building plans.

The ability to access not only the front door but what is inside a building has become a lot easier since the passage of the Americans with Disabilities Act in 1990. It requires that public and commercial buildings accommodate people with limited physical abilities, particularly those who use a wheelchair.

The Center for Universal Design offers many publications to help builders meet ADA guidelines, but the one that may be most useful to young people leaving home is the booklet *Tenant's Guide to Apartment Modifications: An Ideal Source Pamphlet to Simple, Low-cost Modifications to Increase Accessibility to Apartments*. This pamphlet presents illustrated ideas for low-cost modifications that are commonly made to rental dwellings, focusing on the three areas where most accessibility problems occur: entrances, bathrooms, and kitchens. It is available for purchase at the center's website: www.design.ncsu.edu/cud/pubs_p/phousing.htm.

Having a home to call your own is the American dream, and that dream includes people with more severe disabilities who need a supported independent living program. It's hard to find facilities that incorporate all the latest in assistive technology and do it at an affordable price, but the Good Shepherd Rehabilitation Network in Allentown, Pennsylvania, is making this dream come true.

In 2003 Good Shepherd built a unique eighteen-unit independent living apartment complex for low-income disabled individuals. While providing greater independence and a better quality of life to its residents, the complex also saves taxpayers money; research shows that it costs $40,000 to $60,000 less per year for each tenant who comes from a special rehabilitation facility. The apartment complex has received national and international attention from the *New York Times*, *Rehab Management* magazine, and TV Tokyo.

"We did it as part of our mission," says Good Shepherd spokesperson Cynthia A. Lambert. "We exist to help people with disabilities maximize their independence—to be as mainstream as they possibly can be. We built this to demonstrate to Pennsylvania and the rest of the country that using technology is more satisfactory to people who live there because they can do things when they want and how they want. We also demonstrated that it is a cost savings to the government."

The Good Shepherd apartments include technology like a lift system with a track switch that runs from the bedroom to the bathroom, to let the resident get to either the toilet or the shower. Each apartment has a low-to-the-ground clothes washer that washes and dries clothes, eliminating the need to transfer clothes to a separate machine.

"We are working with a company to develop a robotic arm for people who cannot grasp, but who can use electronics," Lambert adds. "We are exploring eye-gaze technology to

PREPARE YOURSELF FOR DISASTER

Everyone should think about being prepared for a disaster before it occurs. The National Organization on Disability's Emergency Preparedness Initiative (EPI) says that people with disabilities need to be more self reliant in emergencies. As usual, you will have to be your best advocate. You know your abilities and needs before, during, and after a disaster. You have to plan to meet your own unique circumstances. Start today!

NOD has info you can download on how to get prepared at www.nod.org/index.cfm?fuseaction=Page.viewPage&pageId=11. The brochure *Prepare Yourself: Disaster Readiness Tips for People with Disabilities* will help you identify your resources, make a plan, and create a ready kit and a go bag.

NOD urges everyone to learn about the types of hazards that could impact your community. Find out what emergency plans your community has and make sure those plans consider your specific needs. Make sure you know how you will be notified when a disaster is on its way or is actually occurring.

Make a list of family, friends, personal attendants, coworkers, and service providers who can be part of your plan. Talk to them and ask them to be part of your support network. Try to get at least three people in each place where you spend time, and make sure you have contact information for your support network. If you receive regular services, make a plan with each of your service providers. Learn about their disaster plans and how to contact them in an emergency.

Make an evacuation plan for home, work, and school. Try to find at least two ways to get out of every building. You should prepare a ready kit with supplies you need and a go bag of your most essential items to take with you if you must leave immediately. Items might include: a three-day supply of nonperishable food; a three-day supply of water, medical equipment, and assistive devices; medications; a list of emergency contact information; copies of important documents like your birth certificate, passport, license, insurance information, and proof of address; extra keys; flashlight and radio with batteries; cash and credit or bank cards; personal items like soap; supplies for a service animal; clothes, blankets, and a pillow; white distress flag or glow sticks; and basic first aid supplies. You should also identify your disability-related or health condition by writing it down or wearing medical alert tags or bracelets.

And don't forget a truck to carry it all!

operate a keyboard. We see that as our future—developing and testing technology that increases independence."[8]

THE JOB OF YOUR DREAMS

"Some will succeed and some won't, but it will be because of their abilities, not their disabilities." —Sen. Tom Harkin of Iowa, May 20, 1998, in *Congressional Record*

Katy Sandberg is a social work major with cerebral palsy. "I want to help juvenile delinquents," she says. "Everyone tells me that they are the population that needs the most help, and there are not a lot of people helping them, so I want to try. I just looked for something I wanted to do. If you don't like what you are doing, then why do it?"[9]

Alex McKenzie, who has been in a wheelchair since he was four, plans to form a consulting business with a friend. They want to help people who suddenly find they are rolling through life in a wheelchair learn to handle the challenges of re-creating their lives. "We want to work with people who have recently acquired disabilities," says Alex. "They have to face a period of coping with not being able to do what they used to do. We can help them figure out that there is still a lot they can do—you just have to do it in different ways. Being in a wheelchair doesn't hold you back."[10]

Mich Gerson, a professional and technical communications major at the National Technical Institute for the Deaf at Rochester Technical Institute, loves her major: "Let me start off by saying that I came into RIT as a business major. Looking back, what was I thinking? I wrote all the time growing up—it was my passion. As a matter of fact, I wrote poetry, short stories, autobiographies ('cause we all know my life is soooooooo interesting), scripts. You name it—I dabbled

INDEPENDENT LIVING ISSUES ON THE NAVAJO NATION

Native Americans have the highest percentage of people with disabilities of any group in the United States, according to U.S. Census information.[11]

"It's a huge issue," says Dr. Ellen Rothman, a pediatrician at the Kayenta Health Center in the Navajo Nation in northern Arizona. Rothman treats many teens with physical disabilities. "This is considered to be a frontier area because there are less than eight people per square mile. We have a higher amount of spinal cord injury due to the high rate of alcoholism and inadequate roads, which delay getting health care after an accident."

Rothman says it is not easy having a physical disability on the reservation. "Think of living with no running water, no electricity, and no phone when you are in a wheelchair. Also, once you have a disability on a tribal reservation, there are political issues. When day-to-day life is so hard, disability issues are just under the radar."

Native Americans with disabilities can be caught between the U.S. federal government's priority of protecting the civil rights it guarantees to all people with disabilities and the tribal leadership's priority of protecting its right to self-government.[12]

"In effect, none of the ADA applies to reservations. Our tribal chapter house has a dirt parking lot with a step, not a ramp, to get inside, and it doesn't have an accessible restroom. This excludes people with disabilities from the local government process," says Rothman.

"There are so many issues facing these kids," Rothman continues. "It's a challenging time of life to go through this as you are coming into your adult body and going through these other changes at the same time."[13]

Rothman decided to start a wheelchair basketball team. "Basketball is a big thing on the reservation. High school games pull in five thousand spectators." Rothman applied for a grant from the Christopher Reeve Foundation and got enough money to buy ten athletic wheelchairs. In 2005 the Mustangs Wheelchair Basketball Team was formed and gave its first demonstration at halftime during a high school game.

One of Rothman's patients is sixteen-year-old Marcus Cly:

> I'm paralyzed from my waist down. I can't walk. In 2004 I was in a car rollover, and I went out the window and twenty-five

(*continued*)

INDEPENDENT LIVING ISSUES ON THE NAVAJO NATION (*continued*)

feet in the air. I damaged my head and side, and my spinal cord broke. I woke up from a coma two weeks later and stayed in the hospital for a month and a half, and then I went to rehab and stayed there for another month and a half. I started doing my exercise and weightlifting, and I'm getting stronger. I'm back to going to school full days again. The school doors don't have the special buttons that automatically open for wheelchair people like you see in town. I open doors myself, or sometimes a teacher can open a door.

The worst part? For me, it's boring. Staying home when I see other people walking out there. I can get around my house myself. I usually stay in my room and listen to music, or I'm in the living room watching TV. It kind of leaves you out of the fun and hurts you every day. Back and forth and in and out of the house. I try to figure out something to do. I fix bikes for my friends.

I've got my wheelchair customized. It's like an off-road wheelchair. The wheels have good tread, like a mountain bike, and it has shock absorbers under my seat. I go around the big block for the fun of it. Friends come up, and I can talk to them. When my friends joke about me, I joke back. I have friends I can laugh with. Sometimes I cruise up to my cousin's house and mess around over there.

I was a cross-country runner—running through the rocks, down hills, up hills. Now I challenge myself every day with my weights. There are a lot of sports I want to try, like hockey, basketball, tennis, and wheelchair racing. It's all about patience. You have to believe in yourself, and you'll be doing what you want to do.[14]

in it. After getting a 1.8 grade point average in business, I quickly switched to communications. Since then, I've always kept my GPA above 3.0. I haven't declared my technical focus, but I want it to be either advertising, women's studies, or creative writing. What do I want to do? Everything. I want to have my own column in all my favorite magazines and newspapers. I want to publish books. I want to get on the *New York Times* best-seller list. I want to be a professor of communications or creative writing."[15]

Rebecca Wylie, a quadriplegic student at the University of Missouri, Columbia, has always been artistic. She manages her college education with the help of four part-time assistants whom she hired herself. The development of computer graphics is opening the door for her to a career in graphic design.

"I've got enough hand movement in my left hand to operate the joystick on my wheelchair," Rebecca says. "I can dial the phone. I can operate the computer. Next semester, I'm taking art classes, and I'll do that with my mouth stick."[16]

Will any or all of these young people achieve their goals? The landmark disability survey released in 2004 by the National Organization on Disability painted a dark picture of the prospects for people with disabilities. It states that three times as many people with disabilities live in poverty, with annual household incomes below $15,000, compared to their nondisabled counterparts (26 percent versus 9 percent).[17] But these circumstances are improving. The U.S. Department of Education says that in 2003, 70 percent of students with disabilities who had been out of school for up to two years had paying jobs, compared to only 55 percent in 1987.[18]

Building job skills. Photo courtesy of the National Technical Institute for the Deaf at Rochester Institute of Technology.

HOW TO PRESENT YOUR BEST IMAGE

Karen McCulloh of the National Organization of Nurses with Disabilities has vision and hearing disabilities as well as multiple sclerosis, and she works full time as the director of a Nonverbal Communication Skills Program to help job applicants present their best image.

"Teens need to be educated in communication effectiveness," says McCulloh. "It will enhance their proficiency and confidence so that when they go out there, they are ready to take on the world. It's a serious issue. Two-thirds of communication is nonverbal—the sound of your voice, the use of your face, your distance, posture, touch, eye behaviors, gestures, and personal appearance."

McCulloh urges teens, "Take every possible course in communications while you are in high school, and in the process, you need to heighten your sense of nonverbal communication. To make a great first impression, you need to make the most of your voice and personal appearance. That's the way it is. People will remember the sound of your voice more than what you said, and they will definitely remember your personal appearance."

McCulloh offers four tips for you to remember when you are meeting with a potential employer. The same tips will work in interactions with many other people, from store clerks to good buddies.

- Eye Contact. Eye contact demonstrates that you are being open and interested. If you are visually impaired, you can simulate good eye contact behavior. Orienting your face in the direction of the person to whom you are speaking is an extremely important skill.

  People who are listening usually try to make more eye contact than people who are speaking. In this way, eye contact regulates whose turn it is to speak. If you are sight impaired and are part of a group, move your head around in a scanning manner so that your head isn't frozen.
- Head Nods. This gesture conveys positive energy, interest, and affirmation. If you are visually impaired, get some feedback from friends or parents to make sure you are nodding and not bobbing.
- Genuine Smiles. Don't smile all the time. A constant smile seems artificial. Your smile will have more impact if you use it to emphasize agreement and amusement.

HOW TO PRESENT YOUR BEST IMAGE (*continued*)

- **Quick Answers. Try to think before you speak, but think fast. Long delays don't make a good impression.**

"Remember," says McCulloh, "interviewers are looking at your leadership potential, sociability potential as well as technical qualifications for the job."[19]

Despite the odds, there are many resources out there to help you plan your future, declare your independence and help turn your dream job into a reality.

RESOURCES

360: The Accessible Lifestyle is an interactive e-zine that challenges the traditional views of people in wheelchairs. You've waited long enough for a magazine that matches your active lifestyle. www.360mag.com/about_us.cfm

AFB CareerConnect is a free resource for people to learn about the range and diversity of the jobs performed throughout the United States and Canada by adults who are blind or visually impaired. www.afb.org/CareerConnect

The Bureau of Labor Statistics offers a great website where young people can explore career information. www.bls.gov/k12

Directory of Independent Living Centers. Click your state on this cool map, and it will show you the nearest center. www.ilru.org/html/publications/directory/index.html

Federal and State Vocational Rehabilitation Programs. Every state has a federally funded agency that administers vocational rehabilitation, supported employment, and independent living services. The services can vary widely from state to state. You may be able to get counseling and guidance, referrals to other agencies, vocational training, interpreter and reader services, rehabilitation technology services and help in finding a job. To find the vocational rehabilitation program in your state, the

REMOVING BARRIERS TO EMPLOYMENT AT THE USGS

The U.S. Geological Survey (USGS) opened its Disability Resource Center, according to its Office of Communication, the first accessible science laboratory in the federal government in the D.C. area, in 2003. The state-of-the-art facility demonstrates the latest advances in assistive technology and ergonomic solutions for the workplace and is designed to ensure that all employees have equal access to professional opportunities at USGS. The center features five workstations with specialized communications and technology solutions for a range of disabilities, including teletypewriters, screen reading and magnification software, a Braille embosser, speech recognition software, and software for optical character recognition and word prediction. The Disability Resource Center will assist supervisors of new employees with disabilities and current employees who become disabled.[20]

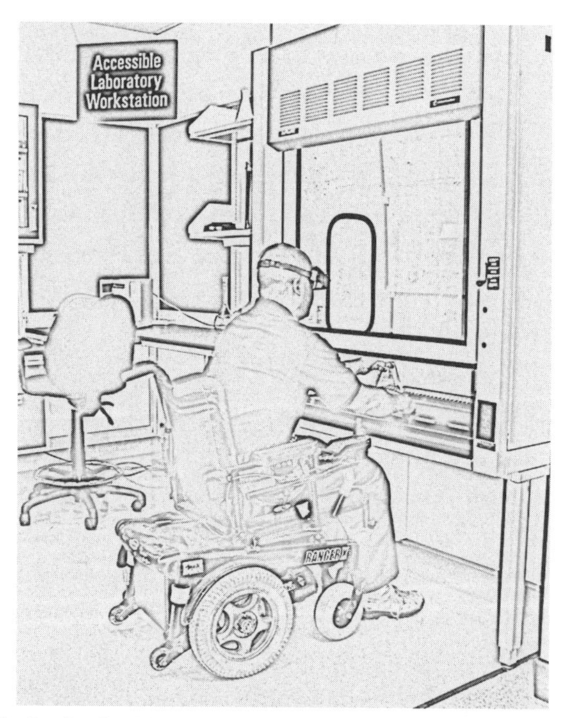

The U.S. Geological Survey (USGS) opened its Disability Resource Center on March 24, 2003, in Reston, Virginia. Courtesy of USGS.

Disability Resources Monthly Guide website has good directory. www.disabilityresources.org/DRMreg.html

JobAccess. The goal of JobAccess is to enable people with disabilities to enhance their professional lives with a dedicated system for finding employment. JobAccess is a place where people with disabilities can seek employment and be evaluated solely on their skills and experience. The JobAccess Résumé Builder helps you to build and post a professional-looking résumé that companies across the United States will be able to browse. www.jobaccess.org

The Job Accommodation Network is a free service of the Office of Disability Employment Policy, U.S. Department of Labor. www.jan.wvu.edu

The National Collaborative on Workforce and Disability for Youth (NCWD/Youth) helps state and local workforce development systems to better serve youth with disabilities. They partner with experts in disability, education, employment, and workforce development to ensure you will be provided with the highest quality, most relevant information available. www.ncwd-youth.info

The National Dissemination Center for Children with Disabilities (NICHCY) has put together a resource called Employment 101 to use as a springboard into the deep ocean of info on employment. You will find most of the resources listed on its website, plus many more. www.nichcy.org/enews/foundations/employment101.asp

The National Organization on Disability (NOD) website is dedicated to expanding the participation of all America's 54 million men, women, and children with disabilities in all aspects of life. Learn here how to close the participation gap. www.nod.org

New Career Paths for Students with Disabilities. Opportunities in science, technology, engineering, and mathematics. ehrweb.aaas.org/entrypoint/paths/index.html

The Office of Disability Employment Policy (ODEP), Department of Labor, is an excellent place to begin understanding the network that can help you find your dream job. ODEP provides information, training and technical assistance to America's business leaders, organized labor, rehabilitation and other service providers, advocacy organizations, families, and individuals with disabilities. www.dol.gov/odep

Partners in Employment is a self-study course designed to help people with developmental disabilities find meaningful jobs and jump-start their careers. Lots of information here, not the least of which are practical skills such as assessing abilities and interests, writing resumes, and preparing for interviews. www.partnersinpolicymaking .com/employment

The Rehabilitation Services Administration (RSA) is a federal agency for assisting eligible people with disabilities to define a suitable employment goal and become employed. You may be able to find medical, therapeutic, counseling, education, training, and other services to help prepare you for work. This is an excellent place for young people and adults with disabilities to begin exploring training and support service options. The RSA funds state vocational rehabilitation agencies. You can find a directory of state vocational rehabilitation offices at this website. www.jan.wvu.edu/sbses/vocrehab.htm

Start on Success. The National Organization on Disability began a pilot project of matching high school students with job experience in 1994. They now have programs in Alabama, Maryland, Connecticut, Ohio, and Pennsylvania. Students work at internships from ten to fifteen hours a week for eight to thirty-two weeks. www.startonsuccess.org

U.S. Department of Labor provides training, technical assistance, and information to improve access for all in the workforce development system. You'll find info on accommodations and assistive technology, relationships with employers, and job-related supports. www.dol.gov/odep/ncwd/ncwd.htm

Youthhood is a website built to help youth with disabilities plan for the future, courtesy of the National Center on

IF YOU LOVE SCIENCE, ENGINEERING, MATHEMATICS, OR COMPUTER SCIENCE, THIS COULD BE YOUR ENTRY POINT!

Students with disabilities represent a pool of untapped talent that can help meet the future needs of research and industry. To meet the challenge of the competitive global economy, private industry and government research agencies have come together to form ENTRY POINT! This program of the American Association for the Advancement of Science (AAAS) offers internship opportunities in science, engineering, mathematics, and computer science to college and graduate students with disabilities. These paid summer internships allow students to apply their skills in a real-world setting.

Mentors advise the students on future undergraduate coursework, plans for graduate study, and/or employment. In addition to offering competitive salary stipends, the companies and agencies provide assistive technology and other reasonable accommodations.

"We have placed 334 students in internships over ten years," says Laureen Summers, spokesperson for AAAS. "Some of those students have come back for multiple summers, which makes 442 placements so far. We follow up on our interns, and 89 of them are working full time. More are in graduate school. It's very exciting."

Students with disabilities who have demonstrated high motivation, persistence, and achievement in academic areas are placed in internships in research and development throughout the country. This is a chance not only to learn more about your field, but also to experience an environment that may be very different from your hometown or university, and as you learn about other people and other ways of doing things, you will learn more about yourself.

Rodney Stewart, who majored in mechanical engineering at New Mexico State University in Las Cruces, was an ENTRY POINT! intern for two summers at IBM in Research Triangle Park, North Carolina. Upon completion of his BS degree, Rodney, who has a mobility impairment, was hired by IBM to work at its manufacturing facility in Poughkeepsie, New York.

Rob Hill, who majored in mechanical engineering at University of Illinois, Urbana-Champaign, interned at Goddard Space Flight Center and the following summer at Kennedy

(*continued*)

IF YOU LOVE SCIENCE, ENGINEERING, MATHEMATICS, OR COMPUTER SCIENCE, THIS COULD BE YOUR ENTRY POINT! (*continued*)

Space Center. Robert, who has cerebral palsy, now works at Boeing in Seattle, Washington.

The internship at National Oceanic and Atmospheric Administration (NOAA) helped Statira Petersen realize the importance of getting a graduate degree and boosted her confidence. She says, "I hope this internship shows that, yes, I might require the assistance of a wheelchair, but that I am smart and able to do any task that is put in front of me."

Her mentor, Christopher D. Hill agrees. "Statira was a joy to have working in our office this summer," says Hill. "She quickly became part of our everyday operations with no extra efforts on our part. Statira brought fresh new perspectives to projects assigned to her, and her productivity was simply amazing."

Just as students learned to apply classroom knowledge in real-world environments, mentors and managers benefited from contact with the scientists-to-be.

"The ENTRY POINT! Program has opened our eyes to the wealth of courage and talents that can be utilized if we look beyond the students' disabilities," says Usha Varanasi, science and research director at NOAA's Northwest Fisheries Science Center in Seattle. "The students show us that if we give this programming a chance, they will give 200 percent in dedication. They can do almost anything."[21]

ENTRY POINT! has a fantastic website called "Roadmaps & Rampways," which chronicles the journeys of three dozen students from childhood through higher education in science, engineering, or mathematics, and on through their early career decisions. Each has a significant disability. Each took a route that bypassed the statistics and defied the stereotypes. Check it out at ehrweb.aaas.org/entrypoint/rr/index.html.

Secondary Education and Transition. This site is a place where you can actively engage in thinking about what you want to do with the rest of your life. You can use this website to plan for your future right now. www.youthhood.org/youthhood/jobcenter/index.asp

NOTES

1. Angela Kuemmel, interview with author, July 13, 2005.
2. Michael Hineberg, telephone interview with author, October 20, 2005.
3. Luciana Sandobal, interview with author, October 21, 2005.
4. Courtney Glodowski, interview with author, August 29, 1005.
5. Dave Groesbeck, interview with author, October 19, 2005.
6. Katy Sandberg, interview with author, September 22, 2005.
7. Angela Kuemmel, interview with author, July 13, 2005.
8. Cynthia A. Lambert, interview with author, September 13, 2005.
9. Katy Sandberg, interview with author, July 13, 2005.
10. Alex McKenzie, interview with author, August 1, 2005.
11. U.S. Census Bureau, "1997 Survey of Income and Program Participation," www.bls.census.gov/sipp/ (March 22, 2006).
12. National Council on Disability, "People with Disabilities on Tribal Lands, Education, Health Care, Vocational Rehabilitation, and Independent Living," August 1, 2003, www.ncd.gov/newsroom/publications/2003/tribal_lands.htm (23 March 2006)
13. Ellen Rothman, interview with author, March 16, 2005.
14. Marcus Cly, interview with author, March 23, 2006.
15. Mich Gerson, e-mail, October 6, 10, 12, and 16, 2005.
16. Rebecca Wylie, interview with author, October 17, 2003.
17. National Organization on Disability, "Landmark Disability Survey Finds Pervasive Disadvantages," June 25, 2004, www.nod.org/index.cfm?fuseaction=page.viewPage&pageID=1430&nodeID=1&FeatureID=1422&redirected=1&CFID=5338505&CFTOKEN=2857954 (October 17, 2005).
18. U.S. Department of Education, "Students with Disabilities Making Great Strides, New Study Finds," July 28, 2005, www.ed.gov/news/pressreleases/2005/07/07282005.html (October 20, 2005).
19. Karen McCulloh, interview with author, August 21, 2005.
20. U.S. Geological Survey, "Expanding Horizons, Removing Barriers for People with Disabilities at USGS," April 20, 2003, www.usgs.gov/newsroom/article.asp?ID=194 (October 19, 2006).
21. AAAS News Archives, "A Summer of Work and Inspiration for ENTRY POINT! Interns," August 24, 2005, www.aaas.org/news/releases/2005/0824entrypoint.shtml (October 19, 2006).

Advocacy

THE IMPORTANCE OF SELF-ADVOCACY

Self-advocacy skills are important for everyone, and they're especially important if you have a disability. Self-advocacy means acting on your own behalf, without the help of a parent, teacher, or aide. You will need these skills all your life to access the services and support you need, whether you are talking to your high school teacher, your college professor, or your boss.

"From any disability perspective," says Michelle Maloney, a graduate student who is severely hard of hearing, "self-advocacy is really important. Especially going from high school to college or a job, you can't depend on your parents. I had to learn how to explain my disability to others and be comfortable with that. You have to stand up to get what you need."[2]

"In so many cases, especially right now, young people are learning that they have the ability to actually set goals for themselves and facilitate those goals," says Betsy Valnes, executive director of the National Youth Leadership Network (NYLN), an organization focused on developing the next generation of disability leaders. "This is a new development in the disability movement. The youth strand of that movement has insights of its own and specializations of its own, such as how to educate young people with special needs."[3]

Betsy, who is twenty-five, has traumatic brain injury. "I had a brain tumor that was misdiagnosed for about four

"In 1979, nineteen youth with disabilities in Denver, Colorado, parked their wheelchairs in front of two inaccessible city buses to stop them from moving. Their protest started a movement that made public transportation all over the country accessible for people with disabilities. What will YOU do to change the world?"

—ADAPT, a grassroots disability organization that promotes services in the community for people with disabilities[1]

FIGHT THE ATTITUDE

"Bad attitudes may be even more insurmountable to a person with a disability than a million stairs. Most people fail to realize that people with disabilities simply want full inclusion. Yet prevailing attitudes promote segregation and exclusion. Bad attitudes suggest people with disabilities are inept and unworthy to participate in all aspects of community life."

—Michael Hineberg, attendant referral coordinator, IndependenceFirst

years," she says. "When it was finally identified, there were complications during surgery, and other portions of my brain had to be removed. Traumatic brain injury affects people differently. For me, I fatigue pretty easily and I have to use learning strategies.

"Students with disabilities can often be their own best advocates. When you go into a general ed classroom, your teachers have usually not even had a full class in their teacher training on working with a student with disabilities. At best, they have a little bit of textbook knowledge about what it means to work with a young person with a disability, but you have lived it. You know what works and what doesn't. Sometimes the tables have to be turned, and the teacher has to be educated by the student.

"People make assumptions about what our needs are. Sometimes teachers don't know what we need because they haven't been there. We have to get involved in give and take with our teachers. There are ways that students with disabilities can positively influence a general ed classroom.

"I pushed for an inclusive setting, and some of the accommodations that I asked for ended up being given to the entire class. For example, in a math class, because of my disability I had a terrible time remembering the formulas. Is the purpose of learning math to memorize a formula, or know how to use that formula? I asked to have the formulas written on a card. I still had to make the judgments about which formula to use and which variables to go into it. My teacher decided to make this change for the entire class. By the end of the year, a lot of students no longer needed cards because they had used the formulas over and over and they had become ingrained by use—not by quick memorization."[4]

NYLN is defining issues that matter to young people with disabilities. Through a series of conferences, it has decided to focus on education, employment, independent living, health, and wellness. "We've decided these issues need to be focused on," says Betsy. "We are a national youth information center. A big thing of ours is research. Young people with disabilities are creating research objectives. We've done three years of research so far."

The NYLN Research Committee recently completed a group of surveys that will compare the style, design, and definition of leadership among three social categories: young leaders with disabilities, young leaders without disabilities, and young people with disabilities who are not yet leaders. The committee plans to use this information to sculpt

A San Francisco rally in support of Americans with Disabilities Act, which was signed in 1990. Photo by Tom Olin.

programs that can take leadership roles within the disability advocacy movement into general society.

NYLN has built a resource list of young leaders who can participate in state, regional, and national activities, such as speaking at conferences, joining policy groups, mentoring, serving on advisory boards and committees, and providing technical assistance to organizations and agencies. To NYLN, education and research are key.

"When it comes to advocating for change, you need to understand the situation, whether you are in a school, some other institution or employment site," Betsy advises. "What you will advocate depends on the equation you are working with. Observe the situation. Identify what it is you have to advocate for. We really try to support young people by helping them understand their reasons. When you want people to change, whether your basis is legal or moral, you need to be able to support your demands. You will be more influential if you are able to do that."

THE ADA GAME

The ADA Game at www.adagame.org is a fully accessible online game that is easy to play and a powerful training and advocacy tool if you want a painless way to learn about disability policy, personal advocacy, and community leadership.

By answering multiple-choice questions about the Americans with Disabilities Act and how it applies to real-life situations, players earn points that can be applied to individual, group, or community advocacy actions. Players can also discuss advocacy strategies or other ADA and disability-related issues on the discussion boards.

You can play this game anytime, and simulate how advocacy can promote positive changes. The ADA Game was developed by the Southeast Disability and Business Technical Assistance Center and funded by the National Institute on Disability and Rehabilitation Research.

You can learn more about NYLN at nyln.org.

To be successful, you must know what you need—not just what you want. You need to be able to find the person or agency you need to talk to. And finally, you have to understand your rights.

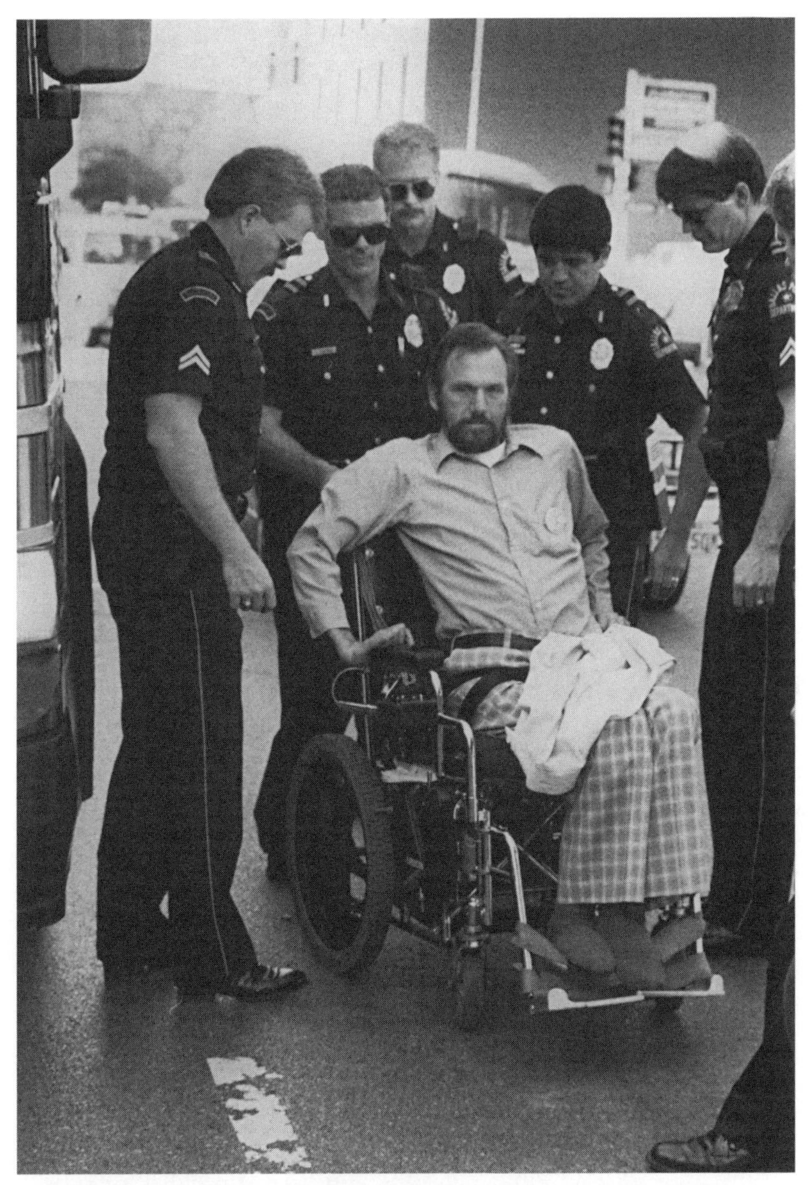

A demonstrator for the passage of the Americans with Disabilities Act being arrested in Dallas. Photo by Tom Olin.

DEFEND YOUR CIVIL RIGHTS

Today we have organizations and legislation designed to help people with disabilities determine the course of their own lives. The independent living movement grew out of the struggle for civil rights for African Americans in the 1950s

DEFEND YOUR CIVIL RIGHTS

You may well ask: "Why direct action? Why sit-ins, marches and so forth? Isn't negotiation a better path?"

You are quite right in calling for negotiation. Indeed, this is the very purpose of direct action. Nonviolent direct action seeks to create such a crisis and foster such a tension that a community that has constantly refused to negotiate is forced to confront the issue. It seeks so to dramatize the issue so that it can no longer be ignored.

—Martin Luther King Jr., Letter from Birmingham Jail, April 16, 1963

and 1960s. Do issues like appalling treatment stemming from prejudice, being stereotyped, and having restricted access to housing, education, transportation, and employment sound familiar? Although people with disabilities weren't included in the 1964 Civil Rights Act, it laid the groundwork for the disabilities rights movement. The ongoing struggle by people with disabilities to gain full citizenship is an important part of our American heritage.

The National Disabled Students Union (NDSU) is a national, cross-disability student organization dedicated to social justice for all. Its mission is to mobilize and organize students with disabilities across the nation to continue that legacy of empowerment and community solidarity. The NDSU is working to ensure that all disabled students have the opportunities they need to learn, the opportunities they need to live and work, and the opportunities they need to be full participants in their communities and full members of American society.

Another organization out there advocating for disability civil rights since 1979 is the Disability Rights Education and Defense Fund (DREDF). Since the passage of the ADA in 1990, DREDF has provided training on this law to more than forty-five thousand people and provides an additional thirteen thousand people a year with information about their legal rights.

Why a defense fund for disability rights? DREDF says there are 49 million people with disabilities living in the United States today. The largest minority in America, people with disabilities are statistically the poorest and least educated.[5] DREDF sees discrimination against people with disabilities occurring every day. Each year it represents clients and assists in cases involving disability rights cases. DREDF has been involved in almost all of the disability rights cases

UNITED NATIONS STEPS IN

With more than 600 million people with disabilities worldwide, a special United Nations committee has begun sessions to create a global convention that promotes equality and non-discrimination of people with disabilities. In a meeting at the UN headquarters in New York on January 25, 2005, Ambassador Luis Gallegos Chiriboga of Ecuador, the chairman of the General Assembly drafting committee, stated:

> **This committee will have direct consequences for those who have to face their life and personal development with a disability. The committee will work to promote and protect the rights and dignity of persons with disabilities, based on the holistic approach in the work done in the fields of social development, human rights and non-discrimination and taking into account the recommendations of the Commission on Human Rights and the Commission for Social Development.**

OBSTACLES TO VOTING

According to the Center for an Accessible Society, access to the voting booth is still a significant problem. One study shows that the voting rate among people with disabilities is 20 percent less than that among nondisabled people, despite state and federal laws—including the ADA—that require polling places to accommodate disabled voters. The Federal Election Commission has reported that more than twenty thousand polling places across the nation are inaccessible, depriving people with disabilities of their fundamental right to vote.

Frequently, polling booths are set in church basements or in upstairs meeting halls where there is no ramp or elevator, in buildings with no disabled parking. This means problems not just for people who use wheelchairs, but for people who use canes or walkers, too. In most states people who are blind don't have the right to a Braille ballot—they have to bring someone along to vote for them.

For more information, visit the Center for an Accessible Society website at www.accessiblesociety.org.

heard by the U.S. Supreme Court. At any given time, DREDF is handling an average of twenty-five cases.

ADAPT is a grassroots disability organization that promotes services in the community for people with disabilities. ADAPT's first issue was access to public transit. ADAPT members fought this civil rights battle for almost a decade, sometimes going to jail in order to achieve equality. Now ADAPT is focusing on federal legislation to change Medicaid so people with disabilities can get medical services in their homes instead of in institutions. They also took on the fight to defend the rights of citizens with disabilities who become displaced by disasters like Hurricane Katrina, which devastated Louisiana and Mississippi in 2005.

ADAPT members are still willing to be arrested to make their point. In September 2005, 500 ADAPT members occupied the offices of congressional leaders, and 104 of them were arrested.

"I think it's important for people with physical disabilities, especially as teenagers, to be able to say 'I want to be a part of society!'" says Jennifer McPhail, an ADAPT organizer who has cerebral palsy. "I can remember when I was a teenager. A lot of things that we have now weren't available. We didn't

After marching to the Capitol, demonstrators left their wheelchairs to crawl to the Senate chambers in support of the Americans with Disabilities Act. Photo by Tom Olin.

have accessibility to schools and the workplace. We fought for those laws, and now we need to insist that the laws passed to protect us actually get enforced.

"Going on a demonstration is an unbelievable awakening. I started on the local level when I was eighteen and the national level when I was twenty. It was great to be with people where I didn't have to explain the frustration that I felt not to be able to enter college or even get access to the public bus system. Demonstrating was an action I could take that would change the way people would perceive my rights. I wasn't just talking about it. I was doing something, and for me, that's what I needed.

"I've been arrested for my beliefs. It is amazingly freeing. I felt like 'I know I'm right—you are not going to get me to change my mind!' The day I got arrested changed the way I carry myself, and people look at me differently. After they put you in jail—what more can they do to you? You have to do what you know is right. The consequences are not going to be greater than the loss of dignity you experience if you do nothing.

MiCASSA: WHERE WILL YOU LIVE?

For decades, people with disabilities, both old and young, have wanted alternatives to nursing homes and other institutions when they need long-term services. Every state that receives Medicaid must provide nursing home services, but community-based services are optional.

MiCASSA establishes a national program of community-based attendant services and supports for people with disabilities. This bill would allow eligible persons, or their representatives, to choose where they receive services and supports. Any individual who is entitled to nursing home or other institutional services would be able to choose where and how these services were provided. The 2 million Americans currently residing in nursing homes and other institutions would finally have a choice.

For an update on how this act is progressing, go to www.adapt.org/casa/update.htm.

"ADAPT is an interesting melting pot. The one thing that defines us is that, until we got together and started changing things, we weren't very respected by society. It's pretty amazing to see five hundred people come together and work so well together. We had five hundred people in D.C. about a month ago. We were there to push the Medicaid Community-Based Attendant Services and Supports Act of 2005 (MiCASSA), and we went to the seven most powerful people in Congress and took over their offices simultaneously and said we would demonstrate until we got commitment on the passage of MiCASSA. They wouldn't give us that, so we got arrested.

"There were some of us who didn't sleep the whole night because we were being processed. As soon as we were out again, we went to the U.S. Department of Housing and Urban Development (HUD) and the HUD director's house. We got a commitment from him that he would meet with us, which is very important.

"I would have loved to have known about ADAPT as a teenager. If you are having a problem—if someone is violating your rights—find the nearest ADAPT chapter, and get involved.

Demonstrating in the 1980s to gain access to public transportation in Los Angeles. Photo by Tom Olin.

"The world we live in now is different than the world I grew up in, and I'm happy about that, but there is still a lot more room for improvement. I encourage young people to get involved now," Jennifer urges. "It's a natural right of passage to confront authority. Fighting for civil rights is a way to take on authority and do something for the betterment of human kind."[6]

TEN LAWS THAT DEFINE YOUR RIGHTS

Historically, as a person with a disability, you face barriers to your schooling and your job prospects. You have been physically blocked from public transportation and services and cut off from telecommunications. The Americans with Disabilities Act and the other laws listed below were created to break down these barriers. People with disabilities aren't the only ones who will benefit as ADA is woven into the fabric of life. Everyone will benefit from living in a society that is made up of the skills and talents of all its individuals.

The ADA gives civil rights protections to individuals with disabilities. It guarantees equal opportunity to you, regardless of any disability, in public accommodations, employment, transportation, state and local government services, and telecommunications.

Since its signing in 1990, this landmark federal law has proved to be a remarkable success; however, it has not fully delivered on its key promise to eliminate discrimination against people with disabilities in the workplace and in public accommodations. Thanks to the ADA, citizens with disabilities are being treated more fairly.

Society is changing how it views and treats its citizens with disabilities. Universal design is the practice of designing products, buildings, and public spaces to be usable by the greatest number of people. Increasingly, we live in an environment of curb cuts, ramps, lifts on buses, and other access designs. Curb cuts designed for wheelchair users also make life easier for people skateboarding, rollerblading, or pushing baby carriages.

Here is an overview of the federal civil rights laws that ensure equal opportunity for people with disabilities.

Americans with Disabilities Act (ADA)

The ADA, signed in 1990, prohibits discrimination on the basis of disability in employment, state and local government, public accommodations, commercial facilities, transportation, and telecommunications.

ADA Title I: Employment

Title I requires employers with fifteen or more employees to provide qualified individuals with disabilities an equal opportunity to benefit from the full range of employment-related opportunities available to others. For example, it forbids discrimination in recruitment, hiring, promotions, training, pay, social activities, and other privileges of employment. It restricts questions that can be asked about an applicant's disability before a job offer is made, and it requires that employers make reasonable accommodation to the known physical or mental limitations of otherwise qualified individuals with disabilities.

Charges of employment discrimination on the basis of disability may be filed within 180 days at any U.S. Equal Employment Opportunity Commission field office. For the appropriate EEOC field office in your geographic area, call (800) 669-4000 (voice) or (800) 669-6820 (TTY) or check out www.eeoc.gov.

ADA Title II: State and Local Government Activities

Title II covers all activities of state and local governments, regardless of the government entity's size or receipt of federal funding. Title II requires that people with disabilities receive an equal opportunity to benefit from all of government programs, services, and activities, such as education, employment, transportation, recreation, health care, social services, courts, voting, and town meetings.

Complaints of Title II violations may be filed with the U.S. Department of Justice within 180 days of the date of discrimination. For information, call (800) 514-0301 (voice) or (800) 514-0383 (TTY), or go to www.ada.gov.

ADA Title II: Public Transportation

Public transportation services, such as city buses and public rail transit may not discriminate against people with disabilities. Paratransit is a service for individuals who are unable to use the regular transit system independently because of a physical or mental impairment, so they are picked up and dropped off at their destinations.

Questions and complaints about public transportation should be directed to the Office of Civil Rights, Federal Transit Administration at (888) 446-4511 (voice/relay).

ADA Title III: Public Accommodations

Title III covers businesses and nonprofit service providers of public accommodations, such as restaurants, retail stores, hotels, movie theaters, private schools, convention centers, doctors' offices, homeless shelters, transportation depots, zoos, funeral homes, day care centers, and recreation facilities like sports stadiums and fitness clubs. Public accommodations must not exclude, segregate, or provide unequal treatment. They must follow architectural standards for new or remodeled buildings; make reasonable attempts to provide communication with people with hearing, vision, or speech disabilities; and remove barriers in existing buildings where it is easy to do without much difficulty or expense.

Complaints of Title III violations may be filed with the Department of Justice. For information, call (800) 514-0301 (voice) or (800) 514-0383 (TTY), or go to www.ada.gov.

ADA Title IV: Telecommunications Relay Services

Title IV addresses telephone and television access for people with hearing and speech disabilities. It requires common carriers (telephone companies) to establish telecommunications relay services (TRS) twenty-four hours a day, seven days a week. This allows callers with hearing and speech disabilities to communicate with others through a communication assistant. Title IV also requires closed captioning of federally funded public service announcements.

For more information about TRS, call the Federal Communications Commission (FCC) at (888) 225-5322 (voice) or (888) 835-5322 (TTY) or go to www.fcc.gov/cgb/dro.

Telecommunications Act

As of 1996 when this act was passed, makers of telecommunications equipment and providers of telecommunications services must ensure that their equipment and services are accessible to and usable by persons with disabilities, if readily achievable. This makes sure people with disabilities have access to products such as telephones, cell phones, pagers, call waiting, and operator services.

For more information, call the FCC at (888) 225-5322 (voice) or (888) 835-5322 (TTY) or go to www.fcc.gov/cgb/dro.

Fair Housing Act

As amended in 1988, the Fair Housing Act prohibits housing discrimination on the basis of race, religion, gender, *disability*, familial status, or national origin. It is unlawful to discriminate in any aspect of selling or renting housing or to deny a dwelling to a buyer or renter because that individual, an individual associated with the buyer or renter, or an individual who intends to live in the residence has a disability.

The Fair Housing Act requires owners of housing facilities to make reasonable exceptions in their policies so that people with disabilities have equal housing opportunities. For example, a landlord with a "no pets" policy may have to allow someone who is blind to keep a guide dog. The act also requires landlords to allow tenants with disabilities to make reasonable access-related modifications to their private living spaces, as well as to common use spaces. The act also requires that new multifamily housing with four or more units be designed and built to allow access for people with disabilities, something you may appreciate when looking for your first apartment.

Complaints of Fair Housing Act violations may be filed with the U.S. Department of Housing and Urban Development. For more information, or to file a complaint, contact the Office of Program Compliance and Disability Rights in the Office of Fair Housing and Equal Opportunity at (800) 669-9777 (voice) or (800) 927-9275 (TTY) or go to the HUD website at www.hud.gov/offices/fheo. For questions about the accessibility provisions of the Fair Housing Act, contact www.fairhousingfirst.org.

Air Carrier Access Act

The Air Carrier Access Act prohibits discrimination in air transportation by domestic and foreign air carriers against qualified individuals with physical or mental impairments. It applies to air carriers that provide regularly scheduled services for hire to the public. The requirements cover boarding assistance and certain accessibility features in newly built aircraft and new or remodeled airport facilities.

For more information or to file a complaint, contact the Aviation Consumer Protection Division at (202) 366-2220 (voice) or (202) 366-0511 (TTY) or go to airconsumer.ost.dot.gov.

Voting Accessibility for the Elderly and Handicapped Act

The Voting Accessibility for the Elderly and Handicapped Act of 1984 requires polling places for federal elections across the United States to be physically accessible to people with disabilities. If no accessible location is available, there must be an alternate means of casting a ballot on Election Day. This law also requires states to provide registration and voting aids, including information by telecommunications devices for the deaf.

For more information, call the U.S. Department of Justice, Civil Rights Division at (800) 253-3931 (voice/TTY).

National Voter Registration Act

The National Voter Registration Act of 1993, also known as the Motor Voter Act, makes it easier for all Americans to exercise their fundamental right to vote. One of the basic purposes of the act is to increase the historically low registration rates of minorities and persons with disabilities that have resulted from discrimination. The Motor Voter Act requires all offices of state-funded programs that are primarily engaged in providing services to persons with disabilities to provide all program applicants with voter registration forms, to assist them in completing the forms, and to transmit completed forms to the appropriate state office.

For more information, contact the U.S. Department of Justice, Civil Rights Division at (800) 253-3931 (voice/TTY).

Civil Rights of Institutionalized Persons Act

The Civil Rights of Institutionalized Persons Act (CRIPA) authorizes the U.S. attorney general to investigate conditions of confinement at state and local government institutions such as prisons, jails, pretrial detention centers, juvenile correction facilities, publicly operated nursing homes, and institutions for people with psychiatric or developmental disabilities. This law allows the attorney general to uncover and correct widespread deficiencies that seriously jeopardize the health and safety of residents of institutions.

For more information, or to bring a matter to the Department of Justice's attention, call (877) 218-5228 (voice/TTY) or go to www.usdoj.gov/crt/split.

Individuals with Disabilities Education Act

The Individuals with Disabilities Education Act (IDEA) requires public schools to make available to all eligible children with disabilities a free public education in the least restrictive environment appropriate to their individual needs. IDEA requires public school systems to develop an appropriate individualized education program (IEP) for each student. The specific education and related services outlined in each IEP reflect the individualized needs of the student.

IDEA also mandates that particular procedures be followed in the development of the IEP. Each student's IEP must be developed by a team of knowledgeable persons and must be reviewed at least once a year. The team includes the student's teacher, the parents, the student, an agency representative who is qualified to provide or supervise special education, and other individuals that the parents or agency may want.

For more information, contact the Office of Special Education Programs, Office of Special Education and Rehabilitative Services at (202) 245-7459 (voice/TTY) or go to www.ed.gov/about/offices/list/osers/osep.

Rehabilitation Act

The Rehabilitation Act prohibits discrimination on the basis of disability in programs conducted by federal agencies, in programs receiving federal financial assistance, in federal employment, and in the employment practices of federal contractors. The same standards apply here as in Title I of the Americans with Disabilities Act.

Section 501

Section 501 requires affirmative action and nondiscrimination in employment by federal agencies of the executive branch.

Section 503

Section 503 requires affirmative action and prohibits employment discrimination by federal government contractors and subcontractors with contracts of more than $10,000.

For more information, contact the Office of Federal Contract Compliance Programs at (202) 693-0106 (voice/relay) or go to www.dol.gov/esa/ofccp.

Section 504

Section 504 states that "no qualified individual with a disability in the United States shall be excluded from, denied the benefits of, or be subjected to discrimination under" any program or activity that either receives federal financial assistance or is conducted by any executive agency or the United States Postal Service.

Requirements include reasonable accommodation for employees with disabilities, program accessibility, effective communication with people who have hearing or vision disabilities, and accessible new construction and alterations.

For information on how to file Section 504 complaints with the appropriate agency, contact the U.S. Department of Justice, Civil Rights Division at (800) 514-0301 (voice) or (800) 514-0383 (TTY) or go to www.ada.gov.

Section 508

Section 508 establishes requirements for electronic and information technology developed, maintained, procured, or used by the federal government. It requires that electronic and information technology is accessible to people with disabilities, including employees and members of the public.

An accessible information technology system is one that can be operated in a variety of ways and does not rely on a single sense or ability on the part of the user. For example, a system that provides output only in visual format may not be accessible to people with visual impairments, and a system that provides output only in audio format may not be accessible to people who are deaf or hard of hearing. Some individuals with disabilities may need accessibility-related software or peripheral devices.

For more information on Section 508, contact the U.S. General Services Administration Center for IT Accommodations at (202) 501-4906 (voice) or (202) 501-2010 (TTY) or go to www.section508.gov.

Architectural Barriers Act (ABA)

The Architectural Barriers Act requires that buildings and facilities that are designed, constructed, or altered with federal funds, or leased by a federal agency, comply with federal standards for physical accessibility. ABA requirements are limited to architectural standards. They do not address the activities conducted in those buildings and facilities. Facilities of the U.S. Postal Service are covered by the ABA.

For information or to file a complaint, contact the U.S. Architectural and Transportation Barriers Compliance Board at (800) 872-2253 (voice) or (800) 993-2822 (TTY) or go to website www.access-board.gov.

RESOURCES

Access Living recognizes that today's youth with disabilities are tomorrow's disability rights leaders. www.accessliving.org/Youth_and_Education.htm

The Americans with Disabilities Act website is a good general source of disability rights information. www.ada.gov

The Center for an Accessible Society's goal is to focus public attention on disability and independent living issues. www.accessiblesociety.org

The Council for Disability Rights advances rights and enhances lives of people with disabilities. www.disabilityrights.org

Disability Rights Advocates is a nonprofit law firm dedicated to protecting and advancing the civil rights of people with disabilities. www.dralegal.org

Disability World is a bimonthly e-zine of international disability news and views. www.disabilityworld.org

Kids as Self Advocates (KASA) is a national grassroots network of youth with disabilities and their friends, speaking out on topics like living with disabilities and health care needs, health care transition issues, school, work, and many more. They also help health care professionals, policy makers, and other adults in our communities understand what it is like to live with disabilities, and they participate in discussions about how to help each other succeed. www.fvkasa.org/index.html

Know Your Rights! at the Alexander Graham Bell Association for the Deaf and Hard of Hearing website explains the civil rights that can protect you from discrimination, whether for school or your professional life, including tips on IDEA, ADA, and self-advocacy. www.hearourvoices.org/DesktopDefault.aspx?p=Rights

The Nth Degree is a site where you can find information, understanding, and solidarity while sharing talent, skills, and stories. www.thenthdegree.com

Ragged Edge is an e-zine full of news items and commentary about issues that concern people with disabilities. www.raggededgemagazine.com

The Smithsonian Museum of Natural History online exhibit on the Disability Rights Movement. Here you can find, photos and audio descriptions of objects and events that tell the story of the Disability Rights Movement at the touch of a button. www.americanhistory.si.edu/disabilityrights/welcome.html

Youthhood is an online community for youth to explore many issues in the youth community and a great place to meet other youth online. www.youthhood.org

NOTES

1. ADAPT, a grassroots disability organization that promotes services in the community for people with disabilities, www.adapt.org/freeourpeople/download/adaptbrain06a.htm (November 28, 2006).

2. Michelle Maloney, interview with author, October 24, 2005.

3. Betsy Valnes, interview with author, October 25, 2005.

4. Valnes, interview with author, October 25, 2005.

5. Disability Rights Education and Defense Fund (DREDF) website, www.dredf.org/what.shtml (February 28, 2006).

6. Jennifer McPhail, interview with author, October 24, 2005.

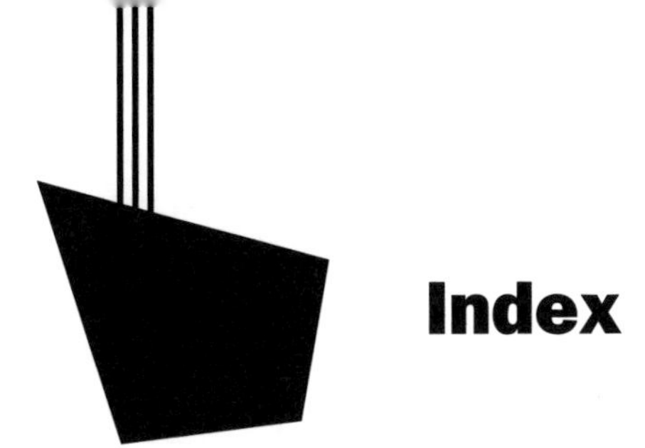

Index

About the Author and Illustrator

ABOUT THE AUTHOR

Denise Thornton is a freelance journalist whose work has appeared in many publications, including feature articles for *Bicycling*, *Electronic House*, the *Wisconsin State Journal*, the *South Bend Tribune*, the *Orlando Sentinel*, and a weekly column for the Lake County Bureau of the *Chicago Tribune*. She recently completed her first middle-grade novel. Denise has a bachelor's degree in journalism from the University of Wisconsin, Madison, where she is currently pursuing a master's degree in science, health and environmental communication. For more than ten years, Denise has been inspired by students who have physical disabilities as she writes and edits the newsletter of the Northern Suburban Special Education District, a cooperative of many school districts on Chicago's North Shore that pool resources to meet the needs of their students with disabilities.

ABOUT THE ILLUSTRATOR

Angelica Busque received her Bachelor of Fine Arts from the School of the Art Institute of Chicago, where she studied experimental sound and video art. In 2001, she began to have health problems that would cause her life to slow down tremendously. By the age of twenty-three, she was hospitalized six times, underwent a splenectomy, and was diagnosed with the autoimmune disease lupus and avascular necrosis that resulted in unbearable hip pain. A total hip replacement allowed Busque to walk again. She also paints and creates art books but is best known for her illustrations in her self-published graphic novel series Morning Star, which has been displayed in both Chicago's Gene Siskel Film Center and at the Smithsonian International Gallery in Washington, DC. Busque is a member of the Day2Alliance artist collective and the International Arts Movement. Currently her lupus is in remission and she enjoys music, dancing—when her arthritis and lupus fatigue allow her to—and watching live stand-up comedy.